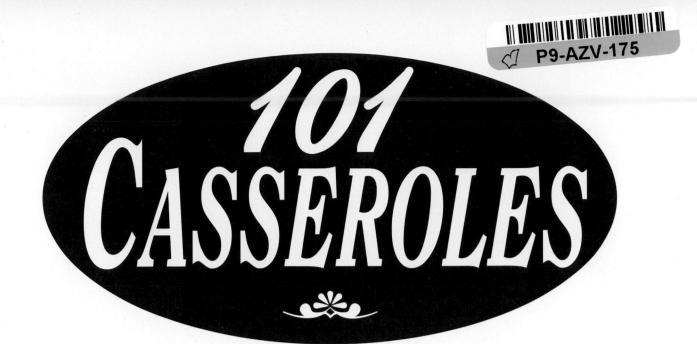

101 CASSEROLES

Publications International, Ltd.
Favorite Brand Name Recipes at www.fbnr.com

Microwave Cooking: Microwave ovens vary in wattage. Use the cooking times as guidelines and check for doneness before adding more time.

101 CASSEROLES

Prime-Time Meats

Steak Pot Pie

1 cup chopped onion
2 tablespoons margarine
3 tablespoons all-purpose flour
1½ cups beef broth
½ cup A.1.® Original or A.1.® Bold & Spicy Steak
    Sauce
3 cups cubed cooked steak (about 1½ pounds)
1 (16-ounce) package frozen broccoli, cauliflower &
    carrot mixture
Prepared pastry for 1-crust pie
1 egg, beaten

In 2-quart saucepan, over medium-high heat, cook onion in margarine until tender. Blend in flour; cook 1 minute more. Add broth and steak sauce; cook and stir until mixture thickens and begins to boil. Stir in steak and vegetables. Spoon mixture into 8-inch square glass baking dish. Roll out and cut pastry crust to fit over dish. Seal crust to edge of dish; brush with egg. Slit top of crust to vent. Bake at 400°F 25 minutes or until crust is golden brown. Serve immediately. Garnish as desired.   *Makes 4 servings*

Steak Pot Pie

Lasagna Beef 'n' Spinach Roll-Ups

1½ pounds ground beef
1 (28-ounce) jar spaghetti
   sauce
½ cup A.1.® Original or
   A.1.® Bold & Spicy
   Steak Sauce
½ teaspoon dried basil
   leaves
1 (15-ounce) container
   ricotta cheese
1 (10-ounce) package
   frozen chopped
   spinach, thawed, well
   drained
2 cups shredded
   mozzarella cheese
   (8 ounces)
⅓ cup grated Parmesan
   cheese, divided
1 egg, beaten
12 lasagna noodles, cooked,
   drained
2 tablespoons chopped
   fresh parsley

In large skillet, brown beef until
no longer pink, stirring
occasionally to separate; drain.
Combine spaghetti sauce, steak
sauce and basil; stir 1 cup
spaghetti sauce mixture into
beef. Set aside remaining
sauce.

Combine ricotta, spinach,
mozzarella, 3 tablespoons
Parmesan and egg. On each
lasagna noodle, spread about

¼ cup ricotta mixture. Top with
about ⅓ cup beef mixture. Roll
up each noodle from short end;
lay each roll, seam side down,
in lightly greased 13×9×2-inch
baking dish. Pour reserved
sauce mixture over noodles.
Sprinkle with remaining
Parmesan and parsley. Bake,
covered, at 350°F 30 minutes.
Uncover; bake 15 to 20 minutes
more or until hot and bubbly.
Makes 6 servings

Baked Ziti with Three Cheeses

8 ounces uncooked ziti
8 ounces sweet Italian
   sausage
1½ cups part-skim ricotta
   cheese
¾ cup (3 ounces) shredded
   ALPINE LACE® Fat Free
   Pasteurized Process
   Skim Milk Cheese
   Product—For
   Parmesan Lovers,
   divided
¼ cup 2% low fat milk
1 large egg white
2 teaspoons minced garlic
3 cups chunky marinara
   sauce
1½ cups (6 ounces)
   shredded ALPINE
   LACE® Reduced Fat
   Mozzarella Cheese

1. Preheat the oven to 375°F. Spray a 14-inch oval au gratin pan or a 13×9×3-inch baking dish with nonstick cooking spray. Spray a medium-size skillet with the cooking spray. Cook the ziti until al dente, according to package directions.

2. Meanwhile, prepare the sausage: Remove the sausage meat from its casing and crumble. Heat the skillet for 1 minute over medium-high heat. Add the crumbled sausage and sauté for 5 minutes or until brown. Transfer to paper towels to drain.

3. In a medium-size bowl, combine the ricotta cheese, ½ cup of the Parmesan, the milk, egg white and garlic.

4. Spread one third of the sauce in the baking dish. Layer with: one half of the ziti, one third of the sauce, all of the ricotta mixture, one half of the sausage, then the remaining ziti, sausage and sauce. Sprinkle with the mozzarella cheese and the remaining ¼ cup of Parmesan.

5. Cover with foil and bake for 45 minutes. Uncover and bake 10 minutes more or until hot and bubbly.   *Makes 6 servings*

Tomato Pesto Lasagna

8 ounces lasagna noodles
1 pound crumbled sausage or ground beef
1 can (14½ ounces) DEL MONTE® Diced Tomatoes with Garlic & Onion, undrained
1 can (6 ounces) DEL MONTE® Tomato Paste
8 ounces ricotta cheese
1 package (4 ounces) pesto sauce
2 cups (8 ounces) shredded mozzarella cheese

1. Cook noodles according to package directions; rinse, drain and separate noodles.

2. Meanwhile, brown meat in large skillet; drain. Stir in tomatoes, tomato paste and ¾ cup water.

3. Layer ⅓ meat sauce, then half *each* of noodles, ricotta cheese, pesto and mozzarella cheese in 2-quart casserole or 9-inch square baking dish; repeat layers. Top with remaining sauce. Sprinkle with grated Parmesan cheese, if desired. Bake at 350°F, 30 minutes or until heated through.
Makes 6 servings

Pork Chops and Apple Stuffing

6 (¾-inch-thick) boneless
  pork loin chops (about
  1½ pounds)
¼ teaspoon salt
⅛ teaspoon black pepper
1 tablespoon vegetable oil
1 small onion, chopped
2 ribs celery, chopped
2 Granny Smith apples,
  peeled, cored and
  coarsely chopped
  (about 2 cups)
1 can (14½ ounces)
  reduced-sodium
  chicken broth
1 can (10¾ ounces)
  condensed cream of
  celery soup, undiluted
¼ cup dry white wine
6 cups herb-seasoned
  stuffing cubes

PREHEAT oven to 375°F. Spray 13×9-inch baking dish with nonstick cooking spray.

SPRINKLE both sides of pork chops with salt and pepper. Heat oil in large deep skillet over medium-high heat until hot. Add pork chops and cook until browned on both sides, turning once. Remove from skillet; set aside.

ADD onion and celery to same skillet. Cook and stir 3 minutes or until onion is tender. Add apples; cook and stir 1 minute. Add broth, soup and wine; stir until smooth. Bring to a simmer; remove from heat. Stir in stuffing cubes until evenly moistened.

POUR stuffing mixture into prepared dish, spreading evenly. Place pork chops on top of stuffing; pour any accumulated juices over pork chops.

COVER tightly with foil and bake 30 to 40 minutes or until pork chops are juicy and barely pink in centers.

Makes 6 servings

Pork Chop and Apple Stuffing

Tortellini Bake Parmesano

**1 package (12 ounces)
fresh or frozen cheese
tortellini or ravioli**
½ pound lean ground beef
**½ medium onion, finely
chopped**
2 cloves garlic, minced
**½ teaspoon dried oregano,
crushed**
**1 can (26 ounces)
DEL MONTE® Chunky
Spaghetti Sauce with
Garlic & Herb**
2 small zucchini, sliced
**⅓ cup (about 1½ ounces)
grated Parmesan
cheese**

1. Cook pasta according to package directions; rinse and drain.

2. Meanwhile, brown beef with onion, garlic and oregano in large skillet over medium-high heat; drain. Season with salt and pepper, if desired.

3. Add spaghetti sauce and zucchini. Cook 15 minutes or until thickened, stirring occasionally.

4. In oiled 2-quart microwavable dish, arrange half of pasta; top with half *each* of sauce and cheese. Repeat layers ending with cheese; cover.

5. Microwave on HIGH 8 to 10 minutes or until heated through, rotating dish halfway through cooking time.

Makes 4 servings

Helpful Hint: For convenience, double recipe and freeze one for later use. This recipe can also be made ahead, refrigerated and heated just before serving (allow extra time in microwave if dish is chilled).

Smoked Sausage and Sauerkraut Casserole

**6 fully cooked smoked
sausage links, such as
German or Polish
sausage (about
1½ pounds), cut into
thirds**
¼ cup packed brown sugar
**2 tablespoons country-
style Dijon mustard or
German-style mustard**
1 teaspoon caraway seeds
½ teaspoon dill weed
**1 jar (32 ounces)
sauerkraut, drained**
**1 small green bell pepper,
stemmed, seeded and
diced**
**½ cup (2 ounces) shredded
Swiss cheese**

Smoked Sausage and Sauerkraut Casserole

1. Place sausage in large skillet with ⅓ cup water. Cover; bring to a boil over medium heat. Reduce heat to low; simmer, covered, 10 minutes. Uncover and simmer until water evaporates and sausages brown lightly.

2. While sausage is cooking, combine sugar, mustard, caraway and dill in medium saucepan; stir until blended.

Add sauerkraut and bell pepper; stir until well mixed. Cook, covered, over medium heat 10 minutes or until very hot. Spoon sauerkraut mixture into microwavable 2- to 3-quart casserole; sprinkle with cheese. Stir sausage into sauerkraut; cover. Microwave on HIGH 30 seconds or until cheese melts.

Makes 6 servings

Prep & Cook Time: 20 minutes

Three Bean and Franks Bake

1 tablespoon vegetable oil
1 medium onion, chopped
2 cloves garlic, minced
1 red bell pepper, seeded and coarsely chopped
1 green bell pepper, seeded and coarsely chopped
1 can (16 ounces) vegetarian baked beans
1 can (16 ounces) butter or lima beans, drained
1 can (16 ounces) red or kidney beans, drained
½ cup ketchup
½ cup packed light brown sugar
2 tablespoons cider vinegar
1 tablespoon HEBREW NATIONAL® Deli Mustard
1 package (12 ounces) HEBREW NATIONAL® Beef Franks or Reduced Fat Beef Franks, cut into 1-inch pieces

Preheat oven to 350°F. Heat oil in large saucepan over medium heat; add onion and garlic and cook 8 minutes, stirring occasionally. Add red and green bell peppers; cook 5 minutes, stirring occasionally. Stir in baked, butter and red beans, ketchup, brown sugar, vinegar and mustard; bring to a boil. Stir franks into bean mixture.

Transfer mixture to 2-quart casserole or 8- or 9-inch square baking dish. Bake 40 to 45 minutes or until hot and bubbly.
Makes 6 servings

Cheesy Beef Enchiladas

1 pound ground beef
1 jar (16 ounces) salsa, divided
2 cups (8 ounces) KRAFT® Natural Shredded Cheddar Cheese, divided
12 (6- to 8-inch) flour tortillas

BROWN meat; drain. Stir in ½ cup salsa and 1 cup cheese.

SPREAD 1 cup salsa in 13×9-inch baking dish. Place ¼ cup meat mixture in center of each tortilla; roll up. Place tortillas, seam side down, on salsa. Top with remaining ½ cup salsa and 1 cup cheese.

BAKE at 350°F for 20 to 25 minutes or until hot.
Makes 6 servings

Three Bean and Franks Bake

Beef Stroganoff Casserole

1 pound lean ground beef
¼ teaspoon salt
⅛ teaspoon black pepper
1 teaspoon vegetable oil
8 ounces sliced
    mushrooms
1 large onion, chopped
3 cloves garlic, minced
¼ cup dry white wine
1 can (10¾ ounces)
    condensed cream of
    mushroom soup,
    undiluted
½ cup sour cream
1 tablespoon Dijon
    mustard
4 cups cooked egg
    noodles
    Chopped fresh parsley
    (optional)

PREHEAT oven to 350°F. Spray 13×9-inch baking dish with nonstick cooking spray.

PLACE beef in large skillet; sprinkle with salt and pepper. Brown beef over medium-high heat until no longer pink, stirring to separate. Drain fat from skillet; set beef aside.

HEAT oil in same skillet over medium-high heat until hot. Add mushrooms, onion and garlic; cook and stir 2 minutes or until onion is tender. Add wine. Reduce heat to medium-low and simmer 3 minutes. Remove from heat; stir in soup, sour cream and mustard until combined. Return beef to skillet.

PLACE noodles in prepared dish. Pour beef mixture over noodles; stir until noodles are well coated. Bake, uncovered, 30 minutes or until heated through. Sprinkle with chopped parsley, if desired.

Makes 6 servings

Beef Stroganoff Casserole

Ortega® Fiesta Bake

1 pound ground beef
1 cup (1 small) chopped onion
¾ cup ORTEGA® Garden Style Salsa, mild
1 package (1¼ ounces) ORTEGA® Taco Seasoning Mix
¼ cup water
1 cup whole kernel corn
1 can (2¼ ounces) sliced ripe olives, drained
1 package (8½ ounces) corn muffin mix, plus ingredients to prepare mix
1 cup (4 ounces) shredded Cheddar cheese
½ cup (4-ounce can) ORTEGA® Diced Green Chiles

COOK beef and onion in medium skillet over medium-high heat until beef is no longer pink; drain. Stir in salsa, taco seasoning mix and water. Bring to a boil. Reduce heat to low; cook 5 minutes or until mixture is thickened. Stir in corn and olives. Spoon into ungreased 8-inch square baking pan.

PREPARE batter for corn muffin mix according to package directions. Stir in cheese and chiles. Stir until smooth; spread over meat mixture.

BAKE, uncovered, in preheated 350°F. oven for 30 to 35 minutes or until crust is golden brown. Top with additional salsa, if desired. *Makes 6 servings*

Pizza Casserole

1 pound BOB EVANS® Italian Roll Sausage
12 ounces wide noodles, cooked according to package directions
2 (14-ounce) jars pepperoni pizza sauce
2 cups (8 ounces) shredded Cheddar cheese
2 cups (8 ounces) shredded mozzarella cheese
6 ounces sliced pepperoni

Preheat oven to 350°F. Crumble and cook sausage in medium skillet over medium heat until browned. Drain on paper towels. Layer half of noodles in lightly greased 13×9-inch casserole dish. Top with half of sausage, half of pizza sauce, half of cheeses and half of pepperoni. Repeat layers with remaining ingredients, reserving several pepperoni slices for garnish on top of casserole. Bake 35 to 40 minutes. Refrigerate leftovers.
Makes 6 to 8 servings

Main-Dish Pie

Main-Dish Pie

1 package (8 rolls)
    refrigerated crescent
    rolls
1 pound lean ground beef
1 medium onion, chopped
1 can (12 ounces) beef or
    mushroom gravy
1 box (10 ounces)
    BIRDS EYE® frozen
    Green Peas, thawed
½ cup shredded Swiss
    cheese
6 slices tomato

• Preheat oven to 350°F. Unroll
dough and separate rolls.
Spread to cover bottom of
ungreased 9-inch pie pan.
Press together to form lower
crust. Bake 10 minutes.

• Meanwhile, in large skillet,
brown beef and onion; drain
excess fat. Stir in gravy and
peas; cook until heated through.

• Pour mixture into crust.
Sprinkle with cheese. Bake 10
to 15 minutes or until crust is
brown and cheese is melted.
Arrange tomato slices over pie;
bake 2 minutes more.

Makes 6 servings

Cheesy Ham Casserole

2 cups fresh or frozen
    broccoli flowerets,
    thawed
1½ cups (6 ounces) KRAFT®
    Natural Shredded
    Sharp Cheddar
    Cheese, divided
1½ cups coarsely chopped
    ham
1½ cups (4 ounces)
    corkscrew pasta,
    cooked, drained
½ cup MIRACLE WHIP® or
    MIRACLE WHIP®
    LIGHT® Dressing
½ green or red bell pepper,
    chopped
¼ cup milk
    Seasoned croutons
    (optional)

• Heat oven to 350°F.

• Mix all ingredients except ½ cup cheese and croutons.

• Spoon into 1½-quart casserole. Sprinkle with remaining ½ cup cheese.

• Bake 30 minutes or until thoroughly heated. Sprinkle with croutons, if desired.
Makes 4 to 6 servings

Prep Time: 15 minutes
Cook Time: 30 minutes

California Tamale Pie

1 pound ground beef or
    ground turkey
1 cup yellow cornmeal
2 cups milk
2 eggs, beaten
1 can (17 ounces) whole
    kernel corn, drained
1 can (14½ ounces) diced
    tomatoes, in juice
1 can (2¼ ounces) sliced
    ripe olives, drained
1 package (1.48 ounces)
    LAWRY'S® Spices &
    Seasonings for Chili
2 teaspoons LAWRY'S®
    Seasoned Salt
1 cup (4 ounces) shredded
    cheddar cheese

In medium skillet, brown ground beef until crumbly; drain fat. In 2½-quart casserole, combine cornmeal, milk and eggs; mix well. Add meat and remaining ingredients except cheese; mix well. Bake, uncovered, in 350°F. oven 1 hour and 15 minutes. Add cheese and continue baking until cheese melts. Let stand 10 minutes before serving. *Makes 6 servings*

Sausage Tetrazzini

1 pound BOB EVANS®
   Italian Roll Sausage
1 medium onion, chopped
1 red or green bell pepper,
   chopped
1 (16-ounce) can stewed
   tomatoes, undrained
1 (10½-ounce) can
   condensed cream of
   mushroom soup
1 (10-ounce) can
   condensed tomato
   soup
½ pound spaghetti, cooked
   according to package
   directions and drained
½ pound fresh mushrooms,
   chopped
1 teaspoon minced garlic
½ teaspoon black pepper
   Salt to taste
1½ cups shredded Cheddar
   cheese

Preheat oven to 350°F. Crumble
sausage into large skillet. Cook
over medium heat until lightly
browned. Remove sausage.
Add onion and red pepper to
skillet; cook and stir until tender.
Place in large bowl. Stir in
tomatoes with juice, soups,
spaghetti, mushrooms, garlic,
black pepper, salt and reserved
sausage; place in 3-quart
casserole. Sprinkle with cheese;
bake, uncovered, 30 to 35
minutes.
Makes 6 to 8 servings

Festive Stuffed Peppers

1 can HEALTHY CHOICE®
   Recipe Creations™
   Tomato with Garden
   Herbs Condensed
   Soup, divided
¼ cup water
8 ounces extra-lean ground
   beef or turkey
1 cup cooked rice
½ cup frozen corn, thawed
¼ cup *each* sliced celery
   and chopped red bell
   pepper
½ teaspoon Italian
   seasoning
2 green, yellow or red bell
   peppers, cut in half
   lengthwise, seeds
   removed

In small bowl, mix ¼ cup soup
and water. Pour into 8×8-inch
baking dish; set aside. In large
skillet, brown beef over
medium-high heat; drain well. In
large bowl, combine remaining
soup with beef, rice, corn,
celery, chopped pepper and
Italian seasoning; mix well. Fill
pepper halves equally with beef
mixture. Place stuffed peppers
in baking dish. Cover and bake
at 350°F 35 to 40 minutes.
Place peppers on serving dish;
spoon remaining sauce over
peppers.   *Makes 4 servings*

Ever-Pleasing Poultry

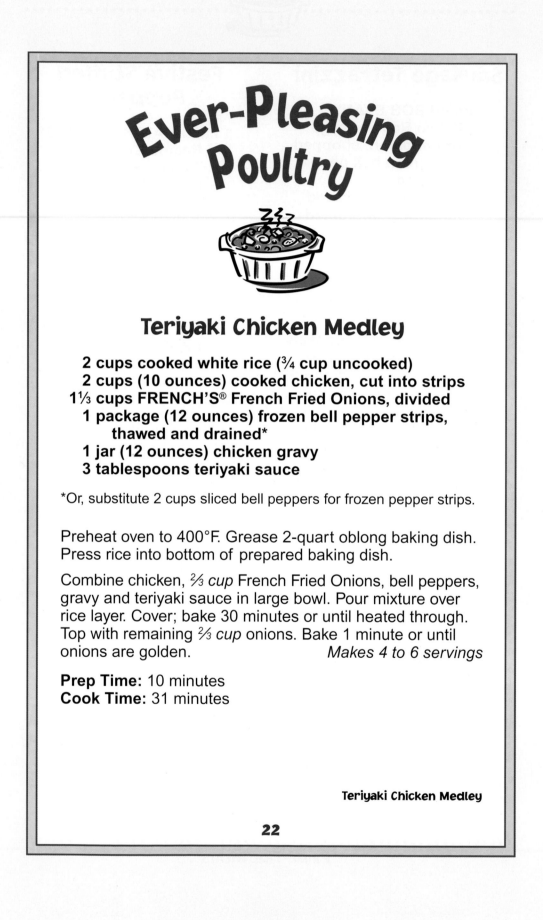

Teriyaki Chicken Medley

2 cups cooked white rice (¾ cup uncooked)
2 cups (10 ounces) cooked chicken, cut into strips
1⅓ cups FRENCH'S® French Fried Onions, divided
1 package (12 ounces) frozen bell pepper strips,
**   thawed and drained***
1 jar (12 ounces) chicken gravy
3 tablespoons teriyaki sauce

*Or, substitute 2 cups sliced bell peppers for frozen pepper strips.

Preheat oven to 400°F. Grease 2-quart oblong baking dish. Press rice into bottom of prepared baking dish.

Combine chicken, ⅔ *cup* French Fried Onions, bell peppers, gravy and teriyaki sauce in large bowl. Pour mixture over rice layer. Cover; bake 30 minutes or until heated through. Top with remaining ⅔ *cup* onions. Bake 1 minute or until onions are golden.   *Makes 4 to 6 servings*

Prep Time: 10 minutes
Cook Time: 31 minutes

Teriyaki Chicken Medley

Turkey Tetrazzini

½ pound fresh mushrooms, sliced
¼ cup sliced green onions
1 tablespoon margarine
2 tablespoons all-purpose flour
¼ teaspoon black pepper
1 (12-ounce) can light evaporated skim milk
⅓ cup low-sodium chicken broth
2 tablespoons sherry (optional)
8 ounces uncooked spaghetti
1 (8-ounce) package HEALTHY CHOICE® Fat Free Shredded Mozzarella Cheese
1 pound turkey breast, cooked, cut into strips

Heat oven to 375°F. Cook mushrooms and green onions in margarine, stirring occasionally, until mushrooms are tender, about 7 minutes. Stir in flour and pepper. Cook and stir 1 minute. Add evaporated milk, chicken broth and sherry, if desired. Cook, stirring occasionally, until sauce is thickened. Remove from heat.

Cook spaghetti according to package directions. Drain, rinse and keep warm. In 2-quart casserole sprayed with nonstick cooking spray, layer half each of spaghetti, cheese, turkey strips and sauce. Repeat layers with remaining ingredients. Bake at 375°F for 25 to 30 minutes or until bubbly and hot.

Makes 6 servings

Savory Chicken and Biscuits

1 pound boneless, skinless chicken thighs or breasts, cut into 1-inch pieces
1 medium potato, cut into 1-inch pieces
1 medium yellow onion, cut into 1-inch pieces
8 ounces fresh mushrooms, quartered
1 cup fresh baby carrots
1 cup chopped celery
1 (14½-ounce) can chicken broth
3 cloves garlic, minced
1 teaspoon dried rosemary leaves
1 teaspoon salt
1 teaspoon black pepper
3 tablespoons cornstarch blended with ½ cup cold water
1 cup frozen peas, thawed
1 (4-ounce) jar sliced pimentos, drained
1 package BOB EVANS® Frozen Buttermilk Biscuit Dough

Savory Chicken and Biscuits

Preheat oven to 375°F. Combine chicken, potato, onion, mushrooms, carrots, celery, broth, garlic, rosemary, salt and pepper in large saucepan. Bring to a boil over high heat. Reduce heat to low and simmer, uncovered, 5 minutes. Stir in cornstarch mixture; cook 2 minutes. Stir in peas and pimentos; return to a boil. Transfer chicken mixture to 2-quart casserole dish; arrange frozen biscuits on top. Bake 30 to 35 minutes or until biscuits are golden brown. Refrigerate leftovers.

Makes 4 to 6 servings

Chicken Parma

4 PERDUE® Individually Frozen™ boneless, skinless chicken breasts
  Salt and ground pepper to taste
1 package (16 ounces) frozen broccoli florets
1 package (6½ ounces) French garlic and herb cream cheese
⅓ cup low-fat milk
4 to 5 slices thinly sliced reduced-fat ham
½ cup Italian-seasoned bread crumbs
3 tablespoons grated Parmesan cheese

Preheat oven to 350°F. Lightly grease 9- to 10-inch square baking dish. Place frozen chicken in baking dish; season with salt and pepper. Arrange broccoli evenly over top.

In small saucepan over low heat, combine cream cheese and milk; cook until smooth and creamy, stirring frequently. Pour half of cream cheese mixture over broccoli; arrange ham slices evenly over top. Pour remaining cream cheese mixture over ham; sprinkle with bread crumbs and Parmesan cheese. Cover and bake 40 minutes. Uncover and continue baking 20 minutes longer, or until chicken is cooked through and topping is golden brown.

Makes 4 servings

Prep Time: 5 minutes
Cook Time: 1 hour

Creamy Chicken Broccoli Bake

4 boneless skinless chicken breast halves (about 1¼ pounds), cubed
1½ cups MINUTE® Original Rice, uncooked
1¼ cups milk
1 package (10 ounces) frozen chopped broccoli, thawed, drained
½ pound (8 ounces) VELVEETA® Pasteurized Process Cheese Spread, cut up
½ cup MIRACLE WHIP® Light® Dressing

MIX all ingredients.

SPOON into 12×8-inch baking dish.

BAKE at 375°F for 30 minutes or until chicken is cooked through. *Makes 6 servings*

Prep Time: 15 minutes
Bake Time: 30 minutes

Turkey & Rice Bundles

1 package LIPTON® Rice & Sauce—Chicken Broccoli
2 cups water
4 turkey cutlets (about 1 pound), pounded thin*
1 jar (7 ounces) roasted red peppers, drained
¼ cup water

*Or, substitute 4 boneless skinless chicken breast halves (about 1 pound), pounded thin.

Preheat oven to 350°F. In medium saucepan, bring rice & sauce—chicken broccoli and 2 cups water to a boil. Reduce heat and simmer, uncovered, stirring occasionally, 10 minutes.

Evenly top each cutlet with roasted peppers; spread with ¼ cup rice mixture. Fold up short sides, overlapping in center, to form bundles. Secure with wooden toothpicks.

In 11×7-inch baking dish, combine remaining rice mixture with ¼ cup water. Arrange turkey bundles over rice mixture. Bake 25 minutes or until turkey is no longer pink in center. Remove toothpicks before serving.   *Makes 4 servings*

Chicken in French Onion Sauce

1 package (16 ounces) sugar snap stir-fry vegetable combination, thawed and drained
1⅓ cups FRENCH'S® French Fried Onions, divided
1 jar (12 ounces) chicken gravy
¼ cup dry white wine
¼ cup water
4 boneless skinless chicken breast halves
Seasoned salt
Cooked white rice (optional)

Preheat oven to 400°F. Grease 2-quart oblong baking dish. Combine vegetables, ⅔ cup French Fried Onions, gravy, wine and water in prepared baking dish.

Arrange chicken breasts over vegetables. Sprinkle chicken breasts with seasoned salt to taste.

Bake, uncovered, 30 minutes or until chicken is no longer pink in center. Stir vegetables around chicken. Sprinkle chicken with remaining ⅔ *cup* onions. Bake 1 minute or until onions are golden. Serve with rice, if desired.   *Makes 4 servings*

Turkey-Tortilla Bake

9 (6-inch) corn tortillas
½ pound 93% fat-free
   ground turkey
½ cup chopped onion
¾ cup mild or medium taco
   sauce
1 can (4 ounces) chopped
   green chilies, drained
½ cup frozen whole kernel
   corn, thawed
½ cup (2 ounces) shredded
   reduced-fat Cheddar
   cheese

1. Preheat oven to 400°F. Place tortillas on large baking sheet, overlapping tortillas as little as possible. Bake 4 minutes; turn tortillas. Continue baking 2 minutes or until crisp. Cool completely on wire rack.

2. Heat medium nonstick skillet over medium heat until hot. Add turkey and onion. Cook and stir 5 minutes or until turkey is browned and onion is tender. Add taco sauce, chilies and corn. Reduce heat and simmer 5 minutes.

3. Break 3 tortillas and arrange over bottom of 1½-quart casserole. Spoon half of turkey mixture over tortillas; sprinkle with half of cheese. Repeat layers. Bake 10 minutes or until cheese is melted and casserole is heated through. Break remaining tortillas and sprinkle over casserole. Garnish, if desired. *Makes 4 servings*

Bayou Chicken Bake

4 to 6 PERDUE®
   Individually Frozen™
   boneless, skinless
   chicken breasts
1½ to 2 teaspoons Cajun or
   Creole seasoning
½ cup chopped onion
1 cup uncooked regular
   long-grain rice
1 package (16 ounces)
   frozen black-eyed peas
2 cans (14½ ounces *each*)
   Cajun-style stewed
   tomatoes
2 tablespoons chopped
   fresh parsley

Preheat oven to 350°F. Lightly grease 13×9-inch baking dish. Sprinkle chicken with Cajun seasoning; place in baking dish. In large bowl, combine onion, rice, black-eyed peas and tomatoes. Pour over chicken. Cover and bake 45 minutes. Uncover and bake 15 minutes longer, or until chicken is cooked through. Sprinkle with parsley before serving.
Makes 4 to 6 servings

Turkey-Tortilla Bake

Lasagna Roll-Ups

1 pound ground turkey
   breast or extra-lean
   ground beef
½ cup chopped onion
2 cloves garlic, minced
1 can HEALTHY CHOICE®
   Recipe Creations™
   Tomato with Garden
   Herbs Condensed
   Soup
1 cup chopped zucchini
¾ cup water
1 (15-ounce) container fat
   free ricotta cheese
½ cup HEALTHY CHOICE®
   Fat Free Shredded
   Mozzarella Cheese
1 egg
4 cooked lasagna noodles

In large nonstick skillet sprayed with vegetable cooking spray, cook turkey, onion and garlic until turkey is no longer pink and onion is tender. Add soup, zucchini and water; simmer 5 minutes. Pour soup mixture into shallow 2-quart baking dish.

In medium bowl, combine ricotta and mozzarella cheeses and egg; mix well. Lay lasagna noodles on flat surface; spread ½ cup cheese mixture on each noodle. Roll up noodles, enclosing filling; place rolls seam sides down over soup mixture.

Cover and bake at 375°F 30 minutes; uncover and continue baking 10 minutes longer or until sauce is bubbly. Place lasagna rolls on serving dish; spoon remaining sauce over rolls.   *Makes 4 servings*

Turkey Green Bean Casserole

1 package (6 ounces)
   STOVE TOP®
   Traditional Sage
   Stuffing Mix
1 can (10¾ ounces)
   condensed cream of
   mushroom soup
¾ cup milk
3 cups cubed cooked
   turkey
1 package (10 ounces)
   frozen French-cut
   green beans, cooked,
   drained

PREPARE stuffing mix as directed on package.

MIX soup and milk in 12×8-inch baking dish until smooth. Stir in turkey and green beans. Spoon stuffing evenly over top.

BAKE at 375°F for 30 minutes or until thoroughly heated.
          Makes 4 to 6 servings

Lasagna Roll-Ups

Mexican Lasagna

4 boneless skinless
   chicken breast halves
2 tablespoons vegetable
   oil
2 teaspoons chili powder
1 teaspoon ground cumin
1 can (14½ ounces) diced
   tomatoes with garlic,
   drained
1 can (8 ounces) tomato
   sauce
1 teaspoon hot pepper
   sauce (optional)
1 cup ricotta cheese
1 can (4 ounces) diced
   green chilies
¼ cup chopped fresh
   cilantro, divided
12 (6-inch) corn tortillas
1 cup (4 ounces) shredded
   Cheddar cheese

PREHEAT oven to 375°F. Cut chicken into ½-inch pieces. Heat oil in large skillet over medium heat until hot. Add chicken, chili powder and cumin. Cook about 4 minutes or until browned, stirring occasionally. Stir in tomatoes, tomato sauce and hot pepper sauce, if desired; bring to a boil. Reduce heat; simmer 2 minutes.

COMBINE ricotta cheese, chilies and 2 tablespoons cilantro in small bowl; mix until well blended.

SPOON half of chicken mixture into bottom of 12×8-inch baking dish. Top with 6 tortillas, ricotta cheese mixture, remaining tortillas, remaining chicken mixture, Cheddar cheese and remaining cilantro. Bake 25 minutes or until heated through.
Makes 6 to 8 servings

Oven Chicken & Rice

1 can (10¾ ounces)
   condensed cream of
   mushroom soup
1 cup long-grain or
   converted rice
1 teaspoon dried dill weed,
   divided
¼ teaspoon black pepper
1 (3-pound) chicken, cut up
   and skinned
½ cup crushed multi-grain
   crackers
1 teaspoon paprika
2 tablespoons butter or
   margarine, melted

Oven Chicken & Rice

PREHEAT oven to 375°F. Combine soup, 1⅓ cups water, rice, ¾ teaspoon dill weed and pepper in 13×9-inch baking dish. Arrange chicken pieces on top of rice mixture. Cover tightly with foil. Bake 45 minutes.

SPRINKLE chicken pieces with crackers, paprika and remaining ¼ teaspoon dill. Drizzle with butter. Bake 5 to 10 minutes or until chicken is tender. Season to taste with salt and pepper.

Makes 4 to 5 servings

Corny Chicken Pot Pies

CHICKEN FILLING
1 tablespoon unsalted
   butter substitute
3 tablespoons all-purpose
   flour
¾ cup low-sodium chicken
   broth
½ cup 2% low fat milk
6 ounces (1 carton)
   ALPINE LACE®
   Reduced Fat Cream
   Cheese with Garden
   Vegetables
¼ teaspoon salt, or to taste
¼ teaspoon freshly ground
   black pepper
2 cups (12 ounces) small
   chunks cooked
   skinless chicken breast
1 package (10 ounces)
   frozen mixed
   vegetables, thawed and
   drained
1 cup (6 ounces) small
   chunks ALPINE LACE®
   97% Fat Free Boneless
   Cooked Ham

CORN BREAD CRUST
1 package (8½ ounces)
   corn bread mix
¼ cup egg substitute or
   1 large egg
⅓ cup 2% low fat milk

1. Preheat the oven to 425°F. Spray six (6-inch) individual au gratin dishes or six (2-cup) baking dishes with nonstick cooking spray. Set aside.

2. To make the Chicken Filling: In a medium-size saucepan, melt butter over medium heat. Whisk in flour; cook 3 minutes, stirring constantly. Gradually whisk in the chicken broth, the ½ cup of milk, the cream cheese, salt and pepper. Cook, whisking occasionally, for 5 minutes or until thickened. Stir in the chicken, vegetables and ham. Cook for 2 minutes or until hot. Divide the filling evenly among the 6 dishes.

3. To make the Corn Bread Crust: In a medium-size bowl, whisk the corn bread mix, the egg substitute (or the whole egg) and the ⅓ cup of milk. (Batter will be slightly lumpy.) Drop heaping tablespoons of batter (about ¼ cup) on top of each of the 6 pies, dividing the batter evenly. Bake, uncovered, for 15 minutes or until the corn bread is golden brown.

Makes 6 servings

Corny Chicken Pot Pies

Chicken Enchiladas

2 cups chopped cooked
   chicken or turkey
1 cup chopped green
   pepper
1 package (8 ounces)
   PHILADELPHIA
   BRAND® Cream
   Cheese, cubed
1 jar (8 ounces) salsa,
   divided
6 flour tortillas (6 inches)
¾ pound (12 ounces)
   VELVEETA®
   Pasteurized Process
   Cheese Spread, cut up
¼ cup milk

STIR chicken, green pepper,
cream cheese and ½ cup salsa
in medium saucepan on low
heat until cream cheese is
melted.

SPOON approximately ½ cup of
chicken mixture down center of
each tortilla; roll up. Place in
lightly greased 12×8-inch
baking dish.

STIR process cheese spread
and milk in small saucepan on
low heat until smooth. Pour over
tortillas; cover with foil.

BAKE at 350°F for 20 minutes
or until thoroughly heated. Top
with remaining salsa. Garnish, if
desired.
   Makes 4 to 6 servings

Turkey Cazuela

8 ounces uncooked
   linguini, broken in half*
1⅓ cups FRENCH'S® French
   Fried Onions, divided
2 cups (10 ounces) cubed
   cooked turkey
1 can (10¾ ounces)
   condensed cream of
   chicken soup
1 jar (8 ounces) picante
   sauce
½ cup sour cream
1 cup (4 ounces) shredded
   Cheddar cheese

*Or, substitute 4 cups cooked pasta
for uncooked linguini.

Preheat oven to 350°F. Grease
2-quart shallow baking dish.
Cook linguini according to
package directions, using
shortest cooking time. Layer
linguini, ⅔ cup French Fried
Onions and turkey in prepared
baking dish.

Combine soup, picante sauce
and sour cream in large bowl.
Pour over turkey. Cover; bake 40
minutes or until hot and
bubbling. Stir gently. Sprinkle
with cheese and remaining ⅔
cup onions. Bake 5 minutes or
until onions are golden.
   Makes 4 to 6 servings

Chicken Enchiladas

Catch of the Day

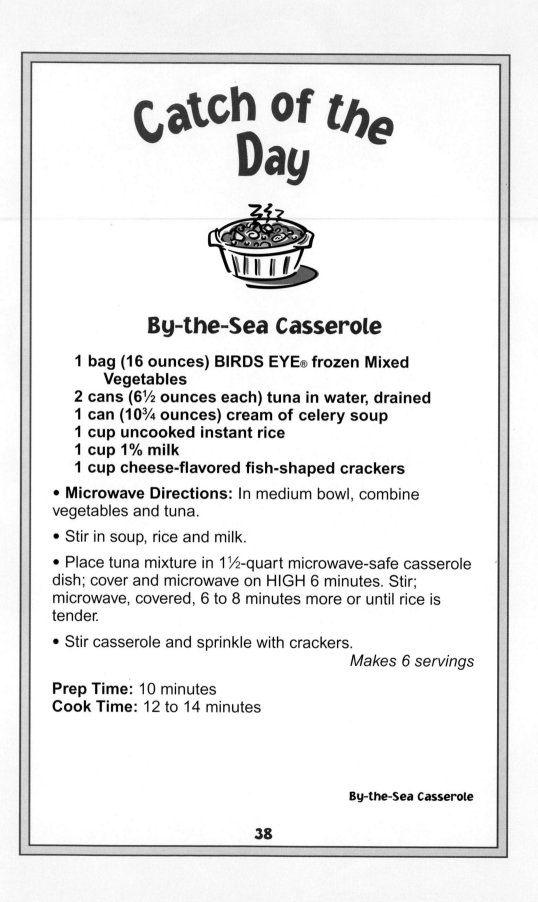

By-the-Sea Casserole

1 bag (16 ounces) BIRDS EYE® frozen Mixed Vegetables
2 cans (6½ ounces each) tuna in water, drained
1 can (10¾ ounces) cream of celery soup
1 cup uncooked instant rice
1 cup 1% milk
1 cup cheese-flavored fish-shaped crackers

• **Microwave Directions:** In medium bowl, combine vegetables and tuna.

• Stir in soup, rice and milk.

• Place tuna mixture in 1½-quart microwave-safe casserole dish; cover and microwave on HIGH 6 minutes. Stir; microwave, covered, 6 to 8 minutes more or until rice is tender.

• Stir casserole and sprinkle with crackers.

Makes 6 servings

Prep Time: 10 minutes
Cook Time: 12 to 14 minutes

By-the-Sea Casserole

Flounder Fillets over Zesty Lemon Rice

¼ cup margarine or butter
3 tablespoons lemon juice
2 teaspoons chicken bouillon granules
½ teaspoon black pepper
1 package (10 ounces) frozen chopped broccoli, thawed
1 cup cooked rice
1 cup (4 ounces) shredded sharp Cheddar cheese
1 pound flounder fillets
½ teaspoon paprika

PREHEAT oven to 375°F. Spray 2-quart square casserole with nonstick cooking spray.

MELT margarine in small saucepan over medium heat. Add lemon juice, bouillon and pepper; cook and stir 2 minutes or until bouillon is dissolved.

COMBINE broccoli, rice, cheese and ¼ cup lemon sauce in medium bowl; spread on bottom of prepared dish. Place fillets on top of rice mixture. Pour remaining lemon sauce over fillets.

BAKE, uncovered, 20 minutes or until fish flakes easily when tested with fork. Sprinkle evenly with paprika.

Makes 6 servings

Lemony Dill Salmon and Shell Casserole

6 ounces uncooked medium shell pasta
1½ cups sliced mushrooms
⅓ cup sliced green onions
1 clove garlic, minced
2 cups skim milk
3 tablespoons all-purpose flour
1 tablespoon grated lemon peel
¾ teaspoon dried dill weed
¼ teaspoon salt
⅛ teaspoon black pepper
1½ cups frozen green peas
1 can (7½ ounces) salmon, drained and flaked

Preheat oven to 350°F. Cook pasta according to package directions. Drain; set aside. Spray nonstick saucepan with nonstick cooking spray; heat until hot. Add mushrooms, onions and garlic; cook and stir until tender. Combine milk and flour until smooth. Stir in lemon peel, dill, salt and pepper. Stir into saucepan; heat over medium-high heat 5 to 8 minutes or until thickened, stirring constantly. Remove from heat; stir in pasta, peas and salmon. Pour into 2-quart casserole. Bake, covered, 35 to 40 minutes.

Makes 6 servings

Flounder Fillets over Zesty Lemon Rice

Potato Tuna au Gratin

1 package (5 or 6 ounces)
    Cheddar cheese au
    gratin potatoes
1 can (12 ounces)
    STARKIST® Solid White
    or Chunk Light Tuna,
    drained and chunked
¼ cup chopped onion
1 package (16 ounces)
    frozen broccoli cuts,
    cooked and drained
¾ cup shredded Cheddar
    cheese
¼ cup breadcrumbs

Prepare potatoes according to package directions. While potatoes are standing, stir in tuna and onion. Arrange cooked broccoli in bottom of lightly greased 11×7-inch baking dish. Pour tuna-potato mixture over broccoli; top with cheese. Broil 3 to 4 minutes or until cheese is bubbly. Sprinkle breadcrumbs over top.   *Makes 6 servings*

Prep Time: 35 minutes

Jambalaya

1 teaspoon vegetable oil
½ pound smoked deli ham, cubed
½ pound smoked sausage, cut into ¼-inch slices
1 large onion, chopped
1 large green bell pepper, chopped
3 ribs celery, chopped
3 cloves garlic, minced
1 can (28 ounces) diced tomatoes, undrained
1 can (10½ ounces) chicken broth
1 cup uncooked rice
1 tablespoon Worcestershire sauce
1 teaspoon salt
1 teaspoon dried thyme leaves
½ teaspoon black pepper
¼ teaspoon ground red pepper
1 package (12 ounces) frozen ready-to-cook shrimp, thawed
Fresh chives (optional)

PREHEAT oven to 350°F. Spray 13×9-inch baking dish with nonstick cooking spray.

HEAT oil in large skillet over medium-high heat until hot. Add ham and sausage. Cook and stir 5 minutes or until sausage is lightly browned on both sides. Remove from skillet and place in prepared dish. Place onion, bell pepper, celery and garlic in same skillet; cook and stir 3 minutes. Add to sausage mixture.

COMBINE tomatoes with juice, broth, rice, Worcestershire, salt, thyme and black and red peppers in same skillet; bring to a boil over high heat. Reduce heat to low and simmer 3 minutes. Pour over sausage mixture and stir until combined.

COVER tightly with foil and bake 45 minutes or until rice is almost tender. Remove from oven; place shrimp on top of rice mixture. Bake, uncovered, 10 minutes or until shrimp are pink and opaque. Garnish with chives, if desired.

Makes 8 servings

Jambalaya

Company Crab

1 pound blue crabmeat, fresh, frozen or pasteurized
1 can (15 ounces) artichoke hearts, drained
1 can (4 ounces) sliced mushrooms, drained
2 tablespoons butter or margarine
2½ tablespoons all-purpose flour
½ teaspoon salt
⅛ teaspoon ground red pepper
1 cup half-and-half
2 tablespoons dry sherry
2 tablespoons crushed cornflakes
1 tablespoon grated Parmesan cheese
Paprika

Thaw crabmeat if frozen. Remove any pieces of shell or cartilage. Cut artichoke hearts in half. Place artichokes in well-greased, shallow 1½-quart casserole. Add crabmeat and mushrooms; cover and set aside.

Melt butter in small saucepan over medium heat. Stir in flour, salt and red pepper. Gradually stir in half-and-half. Continue cooking until sauce thickens, stirring constantly. Stir in sherry.

Pour sauce over crabmeat. Combine cornflakes and cheese in small bowl; sprinkle over casserole. Sprinkle with paprika. Bake in preheated 450°F oven 12 to 15 minutes or until bubbly.
Makes 6 servings

Favorite recipe from **Florida Department of Agriculture and Consumer Services, Bureau of Seafood and Aquaculture**

Broccoli-Fish Roll-Ups

1 can (10¾ ounces) cream of broccoli soup
½ cup milk
2 cups seasoned stuffing crumbs
1 box (10 ounces) broccoli spears, thawed
¾ pound flounder fillets (4 medium pieces)
Paprika

1. Preheat oven to 375°F. Grease 9-inch square baking pan. Combine soup and milk in medium bowl. Set aside ½ cup soup mixture. Combine stuffing crumbs and remaining soup mixture. Pat in prepared pan.

2. Arrange 1 broccoli spear across narrow end of 1 fish fillet. Starting at narrow end, gently roll up fish. Place over stuffing mixture, seam side down.

Repeat with remaining fish and broccoli. Arrange remaining broccoli over stuffing mixture. Spoon reserved ½ cup soup mixture over roll-ups. Sprinkle with paprika.

3. Bake 20 minutes or until fish flakes easily when tested with fork.   *Makes 4 servings*

Baked Fish Galician Style

½ cup plus 4 teaspoons
    FILIPPO BERIO® Olive
    Oil, divided
1 large onion, chopped
2 tablespoons minced
    fresh parsley, divided
2 cloves garlic, crushed
2 teaspoons paprika
1½ pounds new potatoes,
    peeled and cut into
    ⅛-inch-thick slices
1 tablespoon all-purpose
    flour
3 small bay leaves
½ teaspoon dried thyme
    leaves
    Dash ground cloves
4 orange roughy or scrod
    fillets (about 2 pounds)
    Salt and freshly ground
    black pepper
    Lemon wedges (optional)

Preheat oven to 350°F. In large skillet, heat ½ cup olive oil over medium heat until hot. Add onion; cook and stir 5 to 7 minutes or until softened. Stir in 1 tablespoon parsley, garlic and paprika. Add potatoes; stir until lightly coated with mixture. Sprinkle with flour. Add enough water to cover potatoes; stir gently to blend. Add bay leaves, thyme and cloves. Bring to a boil. Cover; reduce heat to low and simmer 20 to 25 minutes or until potatoes are just tender. *(Do not overcook potatoes.)*

Spoon potato mixture into 1 large or 2 small casseroles. Place fish fillets on top of potato mixture. Drizzle 1 teaspoon of remaining olive oil over each fillet. Spoon sauce from bottom of casserole over each fillet.

Bake 15 to 20 minutes or until fish flakes easily when tested with fork. Sprinkle fillets with remaining 1 tablespoon parsley. Season to taste with salt and pepper. Remove bay leaves before serving. Serve with lemon wedges, if desired.
          Makes 4 servings

Tuna Noodle Casserole

1 can (10¾ ounces) condensed cream of mushroom soup
1 cup milk
3 cups hot cooked rotini pasta (2 cups uncooked)
1 can (12.5 ounces) tuna packed in water, drained and flaked
1⅓ cups FRENCH'S® French Fried Onions, divided
1 package (10 ounces) frozen peas and carrots
½ cup (2 ounces) shredded Cheddar or grated Parmesan cheese

Microwave Directions:
Combine soup and milk in 2-quart microwavable shallow casserole. Stir in pasta, tuna, ⅔ *cup* French Fried Onions, vegetables and cheese. Cover; microwave on HIGH 10 minutes* or until heated through, stirring halfway through cooking time. Top with remaining ⅔ *cup* onions. Microwave 1 minute or until onions are golden.

Makes 6 servings

*Or, bake, covered, in 350°F oven 25 to 30 minutes.

Shrimp Casserole

¾ pound raw medium shrimp, peeled, deveined
⅓ cup chopped celery
¼ cup chopped onion
¼ cup chopped green bell pepper
3 tablespoons margarine
1 can (10¾ ounces) condensed cream of celery soup
½ cup dry stuffing mix
1 hard-boiled egg, chopped
⅓ cup sliced water chestnuts
1 tablespoon lemon juice
¼ teaspoon salt
¼ cup (1 ounce) shredded Cheddar cheese

Microwave Directions: Halve large shrimp. In 1½-quart shallow casserole, combine shrimp, celery, onion, pepper and margarine. Cover; cook on HIGH 4 minutes, stirring after 2 minutes. Stir in soup, stuffing mix, egg, water chestnuts, juice and salt. Cover; cook on HIGH 4 minutes. Sprinkle with cheese; cook, uncovered, on HIGH 1 minute.   *Makes 4 servings*

Favorite recipe from **Florida Department of Agriculture and Consumer Services, Bureau of Seafood and Aquaculture**

Tuna Noodle Casserole

Zesty Seafood Lasagna

2 packages (1.8 ounces each) white sauce mix
4½ cups milk
1 teaspoon dried basil leaves
½ teaspoon garlic powder
½ teaspoon dried thyme leaves
¾ cup grated Parmesan cheese, divided
3 tablespoons FRANK'S® REDHOT® Hot Sauce
9 oven-ready lasagna pasta sheets
2 packages (10 ounces each) frozen chopped spinach, thawed and squeezed
½ pound cooked shrimp
½ pound raw bay scallops or flaked imitation crabmeat
2 cups (8 ounces) shredded mozzarella cheese, divided

1. Preheat oven to 400°F. Prepare white sauce according to package directions using milk and adding basil, garlic powder and thyme in large saucepan. Stir in ½ cup Parmesan cheese and RedHot sauce.

2. Spread *1 cup* sauce on bottom of greased 13×9×2-inch casserole. Layer 3 pasta sheets crosswise over sauce. (Do not let edges touch.) Layer *half* of the spinach and seafood over pasta. Spoon *1 cup* sauce over seafood; sprinkle with ¾ *cup* mozzarella cheese. Repeat layers a second time. Top with final layer of pasta sheets, remaining sauce and cheeses.

3. Cover pan with greased foil. Bake 40 minutes. Remove foil; bake 10 minutes or until top is browned and pasta is fully cooked. Let stand 15 minutes before serving.

Makes 8 servings

Prep Time: 30 minutes
Cook Time: 50 minutes

Zesty Seafood Lasagna

No-Fuss Tuna Quiche

1 unbaked 9-inch deep-dish pastry shell
1½ cups low-fat milk
3 extra large eggs
⅓ cup chopped green onions
1 tablespoon chopped drained pimiento
1 teaspoon dried basil leaves
½ teaspoon salt
1 can (6 ounces) STARKIST® Tuna, drained and flaked
½ cup (2 ounces) shredded low-fat Cheddar cheese
8 spears (4 inches each) broccoli

Preheat oven to 450°F. Bake pastry shell for 5 minutes; remove to rack to cool. *Reduce oven temperature to 325°F.* For filling, in large bowl whisk together milk and eggs. Stir in onions, pimiento, basil and salt. Fold in tuna and cheese. Pour into prebaked pastry shell. Bake at 325°F for 30 minutes.

Meanwhile, in a saucepan steam broccoli spears over simmering water for 5 minutes. Drain; set aside. After 30 minutes baking time, arrange broccoli spears, spoke-fashion, over quiche. Bake 25 to 35

minutes more or until a knife inserted 2 inches from center comes out clean. Let stand for 5 minutes. Cut into 8 wedges, centering a broccoli spear in each wedge.
Makes 8 servings

Baja Fish and Rice Bake

3 tablespoons vegetable oil
¾ cup chopped onion
½ cup chopped celery
1 clove garlic, minced
½ cup uncooked white rice
2 cans (14½ ounces each) CONTADINA® Stewed Tomatoes, cut up, undrained
1 teaspoon lemon pepper seasoning
½ teaspoon salt
⅛ teaspoon cayenne pepper
1 pound fish fillets (any firm white fish)
¼ cup finely chopped fresh parsley
Lemon slices (optional)

1. Heat oil in large skillet over medium heat; sauté onion, celery and garlic.

2. Stir in rice; sauté about 5 minutes, or until rice browns slightly. Add tomatoes and juice,

lemon pepper, salt and cayenne pepper.

3. Place fish fillets in bottom of 12×7½×2-inch baking dish. Spoon rice mixture over fish.

4. Cover with foil; bake in preheated 400°F oven 45 to 50 minutes or until rice is tender. Allow to stand 5 minutes before serving. Sprinkle with parsley. Garnish with lemon slices, if desired.   *Makes 6 servings*

Albacore and Spinach Soufflé

2 large eggs, separated
1 cup ricotta cheese
1 package (10 ounces) frozen chopped spinach, thawed and squeezed dry
1 can (6 ounces) STARKIST® Solid White Tuna, drained and flaked
1 tablespoon lemon juice
½ teaspoon *each* Italian herb and lemon pepper seasonings
Whipped Potato Topping (recipe follows)
2 tablespoons melted butter (optional)

In small bowl, beat egg whites until stiff, but not dry. In separate bowl, beat egg yolks and ricotta cheese. Fold in egg whites. In large bowl, combine spinach, tuna, lemon juice and seasonings; carefully fold in egg and cheese mixture. Pour into lightly greased 9-inch pie plate. Spread or pipe Whipped Potato Topping over top, then drizzle with melted butter, if desired.

Bake in 350°F oven 60 minutes. Soufflé should be puffed and golden.
          Makes 6 to 8 servings

Whipped Potato Topping

2½ to 3 cups hot mashed potatoes
¼ to ⅓ cup grated Parmesan cheese
2 to 3 tablespoons light sour cream, if needed

Combine hot mashed potatoes and Parmesan cheese; add sour cream, if necessary, for smooth, creamy potatoes.

Prep Time: 55 to 65 minutes

Bay Village Shrimp

1 pound fresh or thawed
frozen shrimp, shelled
and deveined
1 can HEALTHY CHOICE®
Recipe Creations™
Cream of Celery with
Sautéed Onion & Garlic
Condensed Soup
½ cup asparagus (fresh or
thawed frozen), cut
diagonally into 1-inch
pieces
½ cup sliced mushrooms
¼ cup *each* sliced green
onions and diced red
bell pepper
½ teaspoon dried thyme
½ teaspoon salt (optional)
Vegetable cooking spray
Hot cooked rice
(optional)

In large bowl, combine shrimp,
soup, asparagus, mushrooms,
green onions, pepper, thyme
and salt, if desired; mix well.
Place in 2-quart baking dish
sprayed with vegetable cooking
spray. Cover and bake at 375°F
30 minutes. Serve over rice, if
desired.   *Makes 4 servings*

Egg Noodle-Crab Casserole

12 ounces wide egg
noodles, uncooked
1 can (10¾ ounces)
Cheddar cheese soup
1 cup milk
1 tablespoon minced dried
onions
¼ teaspoon paprika
¼ teaspoon dried marjoram
1 pound crabmeat
1 cup SONOMA Dried
Tomato Halves,
snipped into strips,
parboiled and drained

Cook noodles according to
package directions until al
dente. Set aside and keep
warm.

In medium mixing bowl,
combine soup and milk. Add
onions, paprika and marjoram;
stir. Place noodles in 2½- to 3-
quart casserole. Break up
crabmeat into bite-size pieces;
sprinkle crabmeat and tomatoes
over noodles. Pour soup mixture
over crab mixture; blend well.

Cover and bake in 350°F oven
for 30 minutes or until hot and
bubbly.   *Makes 6 servings*

Bay Village Shrimp

Make It Meatless

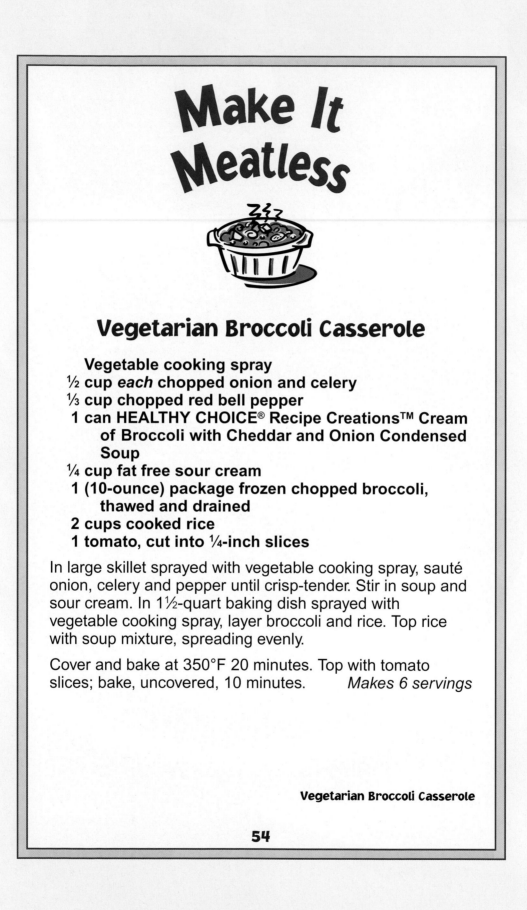

Vegetarian Broccoli Casserole

　　Vegetable cooking spray
½ cup *each* chopped onion and celery
⅓ cup chopped red bell pepper
1 can HEALTHY CHOICE® Recipe Creations™ Cream
　　of Broccoli with Cheddar and Onion Condensed
　　Soup
¼ cup fat free sour cream
1 (10-ounce) package frozen chopped broccoli,
　　thawed and drained
2 cups cooked rice
1 tomato, cut into ¼-inch slices

In large skillet sprayed with vegetable cooking spray, sauté onion, celery and pepper until crisp-tender. Stir in soup and sour cream. In 1½-quart baking dish sprayed with vegetable cooking spray, layer broccoli and rice. Top rice with soup mixture, spreading evenly.

Cover and bake at 350°F 20 minutes. Top with tomato slices; bake, uncovered, 10 minutes.　　*Makes 6 servings*

Vegetarian Broccoli Casserole

54

Chilaquiles

2 tablespoons vegetable
  oil
1 medium onion, chopped
1 package (1.0 ounce)
  LAWRY'S® Taco Spices
  & Seasonings
1 can (28 ounces) diced
  tomatoes, in juice
1 can (4 ounces) diced
  green chiles (optional)
6 ounces tortilla chips
4 cups (16 ounces)
  shredded Monterey
  Jack cheese
1 cup dairy sour cream
½ cup (2 ounces) shredded
  cheddar cheese

In large skillet, heat oil. Add
onion and sauté over medium-
high heat until tender. Add Taco
Spices & Seasonings, tomatoes
and chiles; mix well. Bring to a
boil; reduce heat to low and
simmer, uncovered, 10 to 15
minutes, stirring occasionally. In
lightly greased 2-quart
casserole, layer ½ each of
tortilla chips, tomato mixture
and Monterey Jack cheese.
Repeat layers; top with sour
cream. Bake in 350°F. oven 30
minutes. Sprinkle with cheddar
cheese and bake 10 minutes
longer. Let stand 15 minutes
before cutting into squares.
Makes 6 to 8 servings

Greek Spinach and Feta Pie

⅓ cup butter, melted and
  divided
2 eggs
1 package (10 ounces)
  frozen chopped
  spinach, thawed and
  squeezed dry
1 container (15 ounces)
  ricotta cheese
1 package (4 ounces)
  crumbled feta cheese
¾ teaspoon finely grated
  lemon peel
¼ teaspoon black pepper
⅛ teaspoon ground nutmeg
1 package (16 ounces)
  frozen phyllo dough,
  thawed

PREHEAT oven to 350°F. Brush
13×9-inch baking dish lightly
with butter.

BEAT eggs in medium bowl. Stir
in spinach, ricotta cheese, feta
cheese, lemon peel, pepper and
nutmeg. Set aside.

CUT 8 sheets of phyllo dough in
half crosswise, forming 16
rectangles about 13×8½ inches
each. Cover dough with damp
cloth or plastic wrap while
assembling pie. Reserve
remaining dough for use in
another recipe.

MAKE IT MEATLESS

Greek Spinach and Feta Pie

PLACE 1 piece of dough in prepared dish; brush top lightly with butter. Top with another piece of dough and brush lightly with butter. Continue layering with 6 more pieces of dough, brushing each piece lightly with butter. Spoon spinach mixture evenly over dough. Top spinach mixture with piece of dough; brush lightly with butter. Repeat layering with remaining 7 pieces of dough, brushing each piece lightly with butter.

BAKE, uncovered, 35 to 40 minutes or until golden brown.

Makes 6 servings

57

Curly Macaroni Pie

1 pound uncooked rotini
1 cup seasoned dry bread
    crumbs
½ cup (2 ounces) grated
    ALPINE LACE® Fat Free
    Pasteurized Process
    Skim Milk Cheese
    Product—For
    Parmesan Lovers
½ cup packed fresh parsley
2 tablespoons unsalted
    butter substitute,
    melted
1½ cups chopped red onions
1½ cups coarsely chopped
    red bell peppers
2 cups (8 ounces)
    shredded ALPINE
    LACE® Reduced Fat
    Swiss Cheese
2 cups (8 ounces)
    shredded ALPINE
    LACE® American Flavor
    Pasteurized Process
    Cheese Product with
    Jalapeño Peppers
2½ cups 2% low fat milk
2 tablespoons Dijon
    mustard

1. Preheat the oven to 350°F. Spray a 14-inch oval or round ovenproof baking dish and a large nonstick skillet with nonstick cooking spray. Cook the rotini according to package directions just until al dente. Drain well, place in the baking dish and keep warm.

2. In a food processor, place the bread crumbs, Parmesan, parsley and butter. Process 1 minute or until finely chopped; set aside.

3. Heat the skillet over medium-high heat for 1 minute. Add the onions and bell peppers and sauté for 5 minutes or until soft. Sprinkle over the rotini in the baking dish. Sprinkle with 1½ cups of the bread crumb mixture and the Swiss and pepper cheeses; toss to mix well.

4. In a measuring cup, whisk together the milk and mustard; fold into the rotini mixture until well coated. Top with the remaining bread crumb mixture. Sprinkle with paprika, if you wish. Cover tightly with foil and bake for 50 minutes or until bubbly. Remove the foil and bake 5 minutes more. Transfer to a rack and let stand for 15 minutes. Garnish the pie with fresh parsley leaves, if you wish. Serve hot or warm.

Makes 14 servings

Layered Vegetable Bake

2 slices day-old white bread, crumbled
2 tablespoons chopped fresh parsley (optional)
2 tablespoons butter or margarine, melted
1 large all-purpose potato, thinly sliced
1 large yellow or red bell pepper, sliced
1 envelope LIPTON® Recipe Secrets® Savory Herb with Garlic or Golden Onion Soup Mix
1 large tomato, sliced

Preheat oven to 375°F. Spray 1½-quart round casserole or baking dish with nonstick cooking spray. In small bowl, combine bread crumbs, parsley and butter; set aside. In prepared baking dish, arrange potato slices; top with yellow pepper. Sprinkle with savory herb with garlic soup mix. Arrange tomato slices over pepper, overlapping slightly. Sprinkle with bread crumb mixture. Cover with aluminum foil and bake 45 minutes. Remove foil and continue baking 15 minutes or until vegetables are tender.

Makes about 6 servings

Tuscan Barley Casserole

1 can (16 ounces) kidney beans
1 can (16 ounces) chick-peas
2 cans (8 ounces each) tomato sauce
1 cup quick-cooking barley
1 cup chopped onion
1 cup shredded zucchini
1 cup water
2 teaspoons dried oregano leaves
1 teaspoon dried basil leaves
½ teaspoon garlic powder
¼ teaspoon cayenne pepper
2 tablespoons grated Parmesan cheese
2 tablespoons dried bread crumbs

Preheat oven to 375°F. Drain and rinse beans. Place all ingredients except Parmesan cheese and bread crumbs into 3½-quart casserole. Mix thoroughly. Cover and bake 1 hour. Remove from oven; sprinkle cheese and bread crumbs over top. Return to oven; bake, uncovered, 10 minutes.

Makes 6 (¾-cup) servings

Favorite recipe from **North Dakota Barley Council**

Stuffed Shells Florentine

1 cup (about 4 ounces) coarsely chopped mushrooms
½ cup chopped onion
1 clove garlic, minced
1 teaspoon Italian seasoning
¼ teaspoon ground black pepper
1 tablespoon FLEISCHMANN'S® Original Margarine
1 (16-ounce) container fat-free cottage cheese
1 (10-ounce) package frozen chopped spinach, thawed and well drained
½ cup EGG BEATERS® Healthy Real Egg Substitute
24 jumbo pasta shells, cooked in unsalted water and drained
1 (15¼-ounce) jar reduced-sodium spaghetti sauce, divided

In large skillet over medium-high heat, sauté mushrooms, onion, garlic, Italian seasoning and pepper in margarine until tender. Remove from heat; stir in cottage cheese, spinach and Egg Beaters®. Spoon mixture into shells.

Spread ½ cup spaghetti sauce in bottom of 13×9×2-inch baking dish; arrange shells over sauce. Top with remaining sauce; cover. Bake at 350°F for 35 minutes or until hot.
Makes 8 servings

Stacked Burrito Pie

½ cup GUILTLESS GOURMET® Mild Black Bean Dip
2 teaspoons water
5 low fat flour tortillas (6 inches each)
½ cup nonfat sour cream or plain yogurt
½ cup GUILTLESS GOURMET® Roasted Red Pepper Salsa
1¼ cups (5 ounces) shredded low fat Monterey Jack cheese
4 cups shredded iceberg or romaine lettuce
½ cup GUILTLESS GOURMET® Salsa
Lime slices and chili pepper (optional)

Stacked Burrito Pie

Preheat oven to 350°F. Combine bean dip and 2 teaspoons water in small bowl; mix well. Line 7½-inch springform pan with 1 tortilla. Spread 2 tablespoons bean dip mixture over tortilla, then spread with 2 tablespoons sour cream and 2 tablespoons red pepper salsa. Sprinkle with ¼ cup cheese. Repeat layers 3 more times. Place remaining tortilla on top and sprinkle with remaining ¼ cup cheese.

Bake 40 minutes or until heated through. (Place sheet of foil under springform pan to catch any juices that may seep through the bottom.) Cool slightly before unmolding. To serve, cut into 4 quarters. Place 1 cup lettuce on each serving plate. Top each serving with 1 quarter burrito pie and 2 tablespoons salsa. Garnish with lime slices and chili pepper, if desired.   *Makes 4 servings*

Polenta Lasagna

1½ cups whole grain yellow
    cornmeal
4 teaspoons finely
    chopped fresh
    marjoram
1 teaspoon olive oil
1 pound fresh mushrooms,
    sliced
1 cup chopped leeks
1 clove garlic, minced
½ cup (2 ounces) shredded
    part-skim mozzarella
    cheese
2 tablespoons chopped
    fresh basil
1 tablespoon chopped
    fresh oregano
⅛ teaspoon ground black
    pepper
2 red bell peppers,
    chopped
¼ cup freshly grated
    Parmesan cheese,
    divided

1. Bring 4 cups water to a boil in medium saucepan over high heat. Slowly add cornmeal to water, stirring constantly with wire whisk. Reduce heat to low; stir in marjoram. Simmer 15 to 20 minutes or until polenta thickens and pulls away from side of saucepan. Spread on 13×9-inch ungreased baking sheet. Cover and chill about 1 hour or until firm.

2. Heat oil in medium nonstick skillet. Cook and stir mushrooms, leeks and garlic over medium heat 5 minutes or until vegetables are crisp-tender. Stir in mozzarella, basil, oregano and black pepper.

3. Place bell peppers and ¼ cup water in food processor or blender; process until smooth. Preheat oven to 350°F. Spray 11×7-inch baking dish with nonstick cooking spray.

4. Cut cold polenta into 12 (3½-inch) squares; arrange 6 squares in bottom of prepared pan. Spread with half of bell pepper mixture, half of vegetable mixture and 2 tablespoons Parmesan. Place remaining 6 squares polenta over Parmesan; top with remaining bell pepper and vegetable mixtures and Parmesan. Bake 20 minutes or until cheese is melted and polenta is golden brown.
Makes 6 servings

Polenta Lasagna

Red, White and Black Bean Casserole

2 tablespoons olive oil
1 yellow or green bell
   pepper, cut into ½-inch
   strips
½ cup sliced green onions
1 can (14½ ounces)
   chunky-style salsa
1 can (4½ ounces) green
   chilies, drained
1 package (1½ ounces)
   taco seasoning mix
2 tablespoons chopped
   cilantro
½ teaspoon salt
2 cups cooked white rice
1 can (19 ounces) white
   cannellini beans,
   rinsed and drained
1 can (15½ ounces) red
   kidney beans, rinsed
   and drained
1 can (15½ ounces) black
   beans, rinsed and
   drained
1 cup (4 ounces) shredded
   Cheddar cheese,
   divided
1 package flour tortillas
   (6 inches)

PREHEAT oven to 350°F. Spray
13×9-inch baking dish with
nonstick cooking spray.

HEAT oil in large saucepan over
medium-high heat. Cook and
stir pepper and green onions

about 5 minutes. Add salsa,
chilies, taco seasoning, cilantro
and salt; cook 5 minutes, stirring
occasionally. Stir in rice and
beans. Remove from heat; stir in
½ cup cheese.

SPOON mixture into prepared
baking dish. Sprinkle remaining
½ cup cheese evenly over top.
Cover and bake 30 to 40
minutes or until heated through.
Serve with warm tortillas.
   Makes 6 servings

Vegetarian Lentil Casserole

1 pound lentils, cooked
¾ cup honey
½ cup soy sauce
2 teaspoons dry mustard
1 teaspoon pepper
½ teaspoon ground ginger
½ cup chopped onion
½ cup sliced carrot
½ cup sliced celery
3 tablespoons vegetable
   oil
8 cups cooked white rice

Place lentils in 2½-quart
casserole. Combine honey, soy
sauce, mustard, pepper and
ginger in small bowl. Gently stir
into lentils. Cook and stir onion,
carrot and celery in oil in small
skillet over medium-high heat
until onion is translucent. Add to

lentils. Cover and bake at 350°F 45 minutes. Uncover and bake 15 minutes more. Serve over rice. *Makes 8 servings*

Favorite recipe from **National Honey Board**

Fresh Vegetable Lasagna

8 ounces uncooked lasagna noodles
1 package (10 ounces) frozen chopped spinach, thawed, well drained
1 cup shredded carrots
½ cup sliced green onions
½ cup sliced red bell pepper
¼ cup chopped fresh parsley
½ teaspoon ground black pepper
1½ cups low-fat cottage cheese
1 cup buttermilk
½ cup plain nonfat yogurt
2 egg whites
1 cup sliced mushrooms
1 can (14 ounces) artichoke hearts, drained and chopped
2 cups (8 ounces) shredded part-skim mozzarella cheese
¼ cup freshly grated Parmesan cheese

1. Cook pasta according to package directions, omitting salt. Drain. Rinse under cold water; drain well. Set aside.

2. Preheat oven to 375°F. Pat spinach with paper towels to remove excess moisture. Combine spinach, carrots, green onions, bell pepper, parsley and black pepper in large bowl. Set aside. Combine cottage cheese, buttermilk, yogurt and egg whites in food processor or blender; process until smooth.

3. Spray 13×9-inch baking pan with nonstick cooking spray. Arrange one third of lasagna noodles in bottom of pan. Spread with half each of cottage cheese mixture, vegetable mixture, mushrooms, artichokes and mozzarella. Repeat layers, ending with noodles. Sprinkle with Parmesan.

4. Cover and bake 30 minutes. Remove cover; continue baking 20 minutes or until bubbly and heated through. Let stand 10 minutes before serving.
Makes 8 servings

Layered Mexican Tortilla Cheese Casserole

1 can (14½ ounces) salsa-style or Mexican-style stewed tomatoes, undrained
½ cup chopped fresh cilantro, divided
2 tablespoons fresh lime juice
  Nonstick vegetable cooking spray
6 corn tortillas (6 inches), torn into 1½-inch pieces
1 can (15 ounces) black beans, rinsed and drained
1 can (8 ounces) whole kernel corn, drained *or* 1 cup frozen whole kernel corn, thawed
2 cups (8 ounces) SARGENTO® 4 Cheese Mexican Recipe Blend

1. In small bowl, combine tomatoes, ¼ cup cilantro and lime juice; set aside.

2. Coat 8-inch square baking dish with cooking spray. Arrange ¼ of tortillas in bottom of dish; spoon ¼ of tomato mixture over tortillas. Top with ¼ of beans, ¼ of corn and ¼ of cheese.

Repeat layering 3 more times with remaining tortillas, tomato mixture, beans, corn and cheese.

3. Bake uncovered at 375°F 25 minutes or until cheese is melted and sauce is bubbly. Sprinkle with remaining ¼ cup cilantro. Let stand 10 minutes before serving.

Makes 4 servings

Chili Relleno Casserole

1½ cups (6 ounces) SARGENTO® Light 4 Cheese Mexican Recipe Blend or SARGENTO® Light Shredded Cheese for Tacos, divided
1 can (12 ounces) evaporated skim milk
¾ cup (6 ounces) fat-free liquid egg substitute *or* 3 eggs, beaten
6 corn tortillas (7 inches), torn into 2-inch pieces
2 cans (4 ounces each) chopped green chiles
½ cup mild chunky salsa
¼ teaspoon salt (optional)
2 tablespoons chopped fresh cilantro
  Light or fat-free sour cream (optional)

Chili Relleno Casserole

1. Coat 10-inch deep dish pie plate or 8-inch square baking dish with nonstick cooking spray. In medium bowl, combine 1 cup cheese, milk, egg substitute, tortillas, chiles, salsa and salt, if desired. Mix well; pour into prepared dish.

2. Bake at 375°F 30 to 32 minutes or until set. Remove from oven; sprinkle with remaining ½ cup cheese and cilantro. Return to oven; bake 1 minute or until cheese is melted. Serve with sour cream, if desired. *Makes 4 servings*

67

Breakfast & Brunch Delights

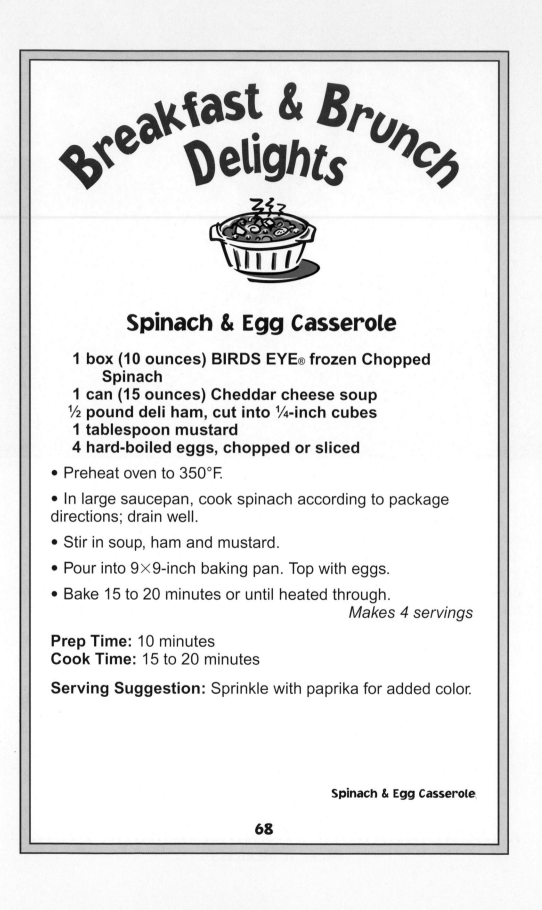

Spinach & Egg Casserole

1 box (10 ounces) BIRDS EYE® frozen Chopped Spinach
1 can (15 ounces) Cheddar cheese soup
½ pound deli ham, cut into ¼-inch cubes
1 tablespoon mustard
4 hard-boiled eggs, chopped or sliced

- Preheat oven to 350°F.

- In large saucepan, cook spinach according to package directions; drain well.

- Stir in soup, ham and mustard.

- Pour into 9×9-inch baking pan. Top with eggs.

- Bake 15 to 20 minutes or until heated through.

Makes 4 servings

Prep Time: 10 minutes
Cook Time: 15 to 20 minutes

Serving Suggestion: Sprinkle with paprika for added color.

Spinach & Egg Casserole

Potato and Egg Pie

1 (20-ounce) package frozen O'Brien hash brown potatoes, thawed
⅓ cup WESSON® Vegetable Oil
1½ tablespoons chopped fresh parsley, divided
1 (12-ounce) package bulk breakfast sausage, cooked, crumbled and drained
¾ cup shredded pepper-jack cheese
¾ cup shredded Swiss cheese
1 (4-ounce) can sliced mushrooms, drained
4 eggs, beaten
½ cup milk
1 teaspoon garlic salt
¼ teaspoon pepper
4 to 6 thin tomato slices

Preheat oven to 425°F. In a medium bowl, combine potatoes and Wesson® Oil; blend to coat. Press mixture into a 10-inch pie dish. Bake for 30 minutes or until golden brown; remove from oven. *Reduce oven temperature to 350°F.* Meanwhile, in a large bowl, combine *1 tablespoon* parsley and *remaining* ingredients *except* tomato slices; blend well. Pour into potato crust. Bake for 25 minutes or until eggs are set.

Place tomato slices over pie and top with *remaining 1½ teaspoons* parsley. Bake 5 to 7 minutes longer.
Makes 6 servings

Spinach and Cheese Brunch Squares

1 box (11 ounces) pie crust mix
⅓ cup cold water
1 package (10 ounces) frozen chopped spinach, thawed and well drained
1⅓ cups FRENCH'S® French Fried Onions
1 cup (4 ounces) shredded Swiss cheese
1 container (8 ounces) low-fat sour cream
5 eggs
1 cup milk
1 tablespoon FRENCH'S® Deli Brown Mustard
½ teaspoon salt
⅛ teaspoon ground black pepper

Preheat oven to 450°F. Line 13×9×2-inch baking pan with foil; spray with nonstick cooking spray. Combine pie crust mix and water in large bowl until moistened and crumbly. Using floured bottom of measuring cup, press mixture firmly into

Spinach and Cheese Brunch Square

bottom of prepared pan. Pierce with fork. Bake 20 minutes or until golden. *Reduce oven temperature to 350°F.*

Layer spinach, French Fried Onions and cheese over crust. Combine sour cream, eggs, milk, mustard, salt and pepper in medium bowl; mix until well blended. Pour over vegetable and cheese layers. Bake 30 minutes or until knife inserted in center comes out clean. Let stand 10 minutes. Cut into squares to serve.

Makes 8 servings

71

Oven Breakfast Hash

2 pounds baking potatoes, unpeeled (5 or 6 medium)
1 pound BOB EVANS® Original Recipe Roll Sausage
1 (12-ounce) can evaporated milk
⅓ cup chopped green onions
1 tablespoon Worcestershire sauce
½ teaspoon salt
¼ teaspoon black pepper
¼ cup dried bread crumbs
1 tablespoon melted butter or margarine
½ teaspoon paprika

Cook potatoes in boiling water until fork-tender. Drain and coarsely chop or mash. Preheat oven to 350°F. Crumble and cook sausage in medium skillet until browned. Drain and transfer to large bowl. Stir in potatoes, milk, green onions, Worcestershire sauce, salt and pepper. Pour into greased 2½- or 3-quart casserole dish. Sprinkle with bread crumbs; drizzle with butter. Sprinkle with paprika. Bake, uncovered, 30 to 35 minutes or until casserole bubbles and top is browned.

Makes 6 to 8 servings

Low Fat Turkey Bacon Frittata

1 package (12 ounces) BUTTERBALL® Turkey Bacon, cooked and chopped
6 ounces uncooked angel hair pasta
1 small onion, sliced
1 red bell pepper, cut into thin strips
2 teaspoons olive oil
1 container (5 ounces) fat-free ricotta cheese
1 cup shredded fat-free mozzarella cheese
1 cup shredded reduced-fat Swiss cheese
4 containers (4 ounces each) egg substitute
½ teaspoon salt
½ teaspoon pepper
1 package (10 ounces) frozen spinach, thawed and squeezed dry
Salsa (optional)

Cook pasta; drain. Sauté onion and bell pepper in oil until tender. Combine cheeses, egg substitute, salt, pepper and pasta. Add vegetables, spinach and bacon. Spray 12-inch quiche dish with nonstick cooking spray; pour mixture into dish. Bake in 350°F oven 30 minutes. Serve with salsa.

Makes 8 servings

Breakfast Bread Pudding with Berry Sauce

8 slices cinnamon raisin bread, cubed
2 cups skim milk
1 cup EGG BEATERS® Healthy Real Egg Substitute
¼ cup sugar
1 teaspoon vanilla extract
½ teaspoon ground nutmeg
½ cup maple-flavored syrup
2 tablespoons FLEISCHMANN'S® Original Margarine
1 cup sliced strawberries
½ cup blueberries
1 teaspoon lemon peel
1 teaspoon lemon juice

Evenly divide bread cubes between 8 greased heatproof (6-ounce) custard cups or ramekins. In medium bowl, combine milk, Egg Beaters®, sugar, vanilla and nutmeg. Evenly pour mixture over bread cubes. Place cups in roasting pan filled with 1-inch depth hot water. Bake at 325°F for 35 to 45 minutes or until set. Let stand for 5 minutes. In small saucepan, heat syrup and margarine until blended. Stir in fruit, lemon peel and juice; heat through. Unmold puddings onto serving plates; serve with berry sauce. *Makes 8 servings*

Oven French Toast

1½ cups packed brown sugar
½ cup butter or margarine
4 eggs
1¾ cups milk
1 teaspoon vanilla extract
1 pound loaf day old Italian bread, cut into 1-inch-thick slices
1 teaspoon ground cinnamon

Preheat oven to 375°F. Place brown sugar and butter in 13×9-inch baking dish; place in oven until butter melts, stirring occasionally. Remove from oven; spread mixture to cover bottom of dish. Whisk eggs, milk and vanilla in shallow bowl until blended. Dip each bread slice into egg mixture, soaking both sides. Set on top of brown sugar mixture in dish. Sprinkle evenly with cinnamon. Bake 20 to 30 minutes or until golden brown. Serve hot, brown sugar sides up. *Makes 8 servings*

Favorite recipe from **Bob Evans®**

Cheesy Country SPAM™ Puff

6 slices white bread, torn
   into small pieces
1¼ cups milk
3 eggs
1 tablespoon spicy
   mustard
½ teaspoon garlic powder
½ teaspoon paprika
1 (12-ounce) can SPAM®
   Luncheon Meat, cubed
2 cups (8 ounces)
   shredded sharp
   Cheddar cheese,
   divided
½ cup chopped onion
½ cup (2 ounces) shredded
   Monterey Jack cheese

Heat oven to 375°F. In large
bowl, combine bread, milk,
eggs, mustard, garlic powder
and paprika. Beat at medium
speed of electric mixer 1 minute
or until smooth. Stir in SPAM®, 1
cup Cheddar cheese and onion.
Pour into greased 12×8-inch
baking dish. Bake 25 minutes.
Top with remaining 1 cup
Cheddar cheese and Monterey
Jack cheese. Bake 5 minutes
longer or until cheese is melted.
Let stand 10 minutes before
serving.   *Makes 6 servings*

SPAM™ Hash Brown Bake

1 (32-ounce) package
   frozen hash brown
   potatoes, thawed
   slightly
½ cup butter or margarine,
   melted
1 teaspoon salt
1 teaspoon black pepper
½ teaspoon garlic powder
1 (12-ounce) can SPAM®
   Luncheon Meat, cubed
1 (10¾-ounce) can cream
   of chicken soup
2 cups (8 ounces)
   shredded Cheddar
   cheese
1½ cups sour cream
½ cup milk
½ cup chopped onion
1 (4.25-ounce) jar
   CHI-CHI'S® Diced
   Green Chilies, drained
2 cups crushed potato
   chips

Heat oven to 350°F. Combine
potatoes, butter, salt, pepper
and garlic powder. In separate
bowl, combine SPAM®, soup,
cheese, sour cream, milk, onion
and chilies. Combine SPAM™
and potato mixtures. Pour into
2-quart baking dish. Sprinkle
with chips. Bake 45 to 60
minutes or until heated.
          Makes 8 servings

Cheesy Country SPAM™ Puff

74

Sausage and Cheese Potato Casserole

1 pound BOB EVANS®
   Italian Roll Sausage
4 cups cubed unpeeled red
   skin potatoes
1 cup (4 ounces) shredded
   Monterey Jack cheese
¼ cup chopped green
   onions
1 (4-ounce) can chopped
   green chiles, drained
6 eggs
¾ cup milk
¼ teaspoon salt
⅛ teaspoon black pepper
½ cup grated Parmesan
   cheese

Preheat oven to 350°F. Crumble
and cook sausage in medium
skillet until browned. Drain off
any drippings. Spread potatoes
in greased 13×9-inch baking
pan. Top with cooked sausage,
Monterey Jack cheese, green
onions and chiles. Whisk eggs,
milk, salt and pepper in medium
bowl until frothy. Pour egg
mixture over sausage layer;
bake 30 minutes. Remove from
oven. Sprinkle with Parmesan
cheese; bake 15 minutes more
or until eggs are set. Refrigerate
leftovers.

Makes 6 to 8 servings

Apple & Raisin Oven Pancake

1 large baking apple, cored
   and thinly sliced
⅓ cup golden raisins
2 tablespoons packed
   brown sugar
½ teaspoon ground
   cinnamon
4 eggs
⅔ cup milk
⅔ cup all-purpose flour
2 tablespoons margarine
   or butter, melted
  Powdered sugar
  (optional)

PREHEAT oven to 350°F. Spray
9-inch pie plate with nonstick
cooking spray.

COMBINE apple, raisins, brown
sugar and cinnamon in medium
bowl. Transfer to prepared pie
plate.

BAKE, uncovered, 10 to 15
minutes or until apple begins to
soften. Remove from oven.
*Increase oven temperature to
450°F.*

WHISK eggs, milk, flour and
margarine in medium bowl until
blended. Pour batter over apple
mixture.

BAKE 15 minutes or until
pancake is golden brown.
Sprinkle with powdered sugar, if
desired.   *Makes 6 servings*

Apple & Raisin Oven Pancake

Betty Jo's Sausage and Cheese Grits

WESSON® No-Stick
  Cooking Spray
1 pound mild or hot
  cooked sausage,
  crumbled and drained
1½ cups grits
2½ cups shredded Cheddar
  cheese
  3 tablespoons WESSON®
  Vegetable Oil
1½ cups milk
  3 eggs, slightly beaten

Preheat oven to 350°F. Lightly spray a 13×9×2-inch baking dish with Wesson® Cooking Spray. Evenly spread sausage on bottom of dish; set aside. Bring 4½ cups water to a boil in a large saucepan. Stir in grits and lower heat. Cook 5 minutes until thickened, stirring occasionally. Add cheese and Wesson® Oil; stir until cheese has melted. Stir in milk and eggs; blend well. Evenly spoon mixture over sausage; bake, uncovered, 1 hour or until grits have set.

Makes 6 to 8 servings

Chile Tortilla Brunch Casserole

2 cans (7 ounces each)
    ORTEGA® Whole Green
    Chiles, split in half
6 corn tortillas, cut into
    strips
4 cups (16 ounces)
    shredded Monterey
    Jack cheese
1 cup chopped tomato
4 tablespoons chopped
    green onions, divided
8 eggs
½ cup milk
½ teaspoon salt
½ teaspoon ground cumin
½ teaspoon ground black
    pepper
    ORTEGA® Thick &
    Chunky Salsa, hot,
    medium or mild

LAYER 1 can chile halves, half of tortilla strips and 2 cups cheese in greased 9-inch square baking pan. Top with tomato and *2 tablespoons* green onions. Layer remaining 1 can chile halves, tortilla strips and 2 cups cheese over tomato. Beat eggs, milk, salt, cumin and pepper in medium bowl; pour over chile mixture.

BAKE, uncovered, in preheated 350°F. oven for 40 to 45 minutes or until center is set. Cool in pan on wire rack for 10 minutes;

sprinkle with *remaining 2 tablespoons* green onions. Serve with salsa.

Makes 8 servings

Egg & Sausage Casserole

½ pound pork sausage
3 tablespoons margarine
    or butter, divided
2 tablespoons all-purpose
    flour
¼ teaspoon salt
¼ teaspoon black pepper
1¼ cups milk
2 cups frozen hash brown
    potatoes
4 eggs, hard boiled and
    thinly sliced
½ cup cornflake crumbs
¼ cup sliced green onions

PREHEAT oven to 350°F. Spray 2-quart oval casserole with nonstick cooking spray. Crumble sausage into large skillet; brown over medium-high heat until no longer pink, stirring to separate sausage. Drain sausage on paper towels. Discard fat and wipe skillet with paper towel.

MELT 2 tablespoons margarine in same skillet over medium heat. Stir in flour, salt and pepper until smooth. Gradually stir in milk; cook and stir until thickened. Add sausage, potatoes and eggs; stir to combine. Pour into prepared dish. Melt remaining 1 tablespoon margarine. Combine cornflake crumbs and melted margarine in small bowl; sprinkle evenly over sausage mixture. Bake, uncovered, 30 minutes or until hot and bubbly. Sprinkle with onions.

Makes 6 servings

Chicken Cordon Bleu Bake

8 slices day-old white or whole-wheat bread, crusts removed
8 thin slices (1 ounce each) ALPINE LACE® Reduced Fat Swiss Cheese
2 tablespoons unsalted butter substitute
¼ cup all-purpose flour
1⅔ cups 2% low fat milk
½ teaspoon freshly ground black pepper
¼ teaspoon salt
12 thin slices (½ ounce each) skinless roasted chicken or turkey
12 thin slices (½ ounce each) ALPINE LACE® 97% Fat Free Boneless Cooked Ham
1 cup thin strips yellow onion

1. Preheat the oven to 350°F. Butter a 13×9×3-inch ovenproof dish. Cut each bread slice into 4 triangles, making 32. Line the bottom of the dish with 16 triangles, overlapping as you go along. Cut the cheese into 4×¼-inch strips.

2. In a medium-size saucepan, melt the butter over medium heat. Stir in the flour and cook until bubbly. Whisk in the milk, pepper and salt. Cook, whisking constantly, for 5 minutes or until slightly thickened.

3. Spread one fourth of the sauce in the baking dish. Layer one third of the chicken, one third of the cheese, one third of the ham, one third of the onion and one fourth of the sauce. Repeat 2 times. Top with the remaining 16 triangles of bread, placing them around the edge and down the center.

4. Bake for 40 minutes or until puffy and golden brown. Let stand for 10 minutes before serving.   *Makes 8 servings*

Vegetable Sides & More

Baked Tomato Risotto

2 medium zucchini
1 jar (28 ounces) spaghetti sauce
1 can (14 ounces) chicken broth
1 can (4 ounces) sliced mushrooms
1 cup arborio rice
2 cups (8 ounces) shredded mozzarella cheese
  Yellow bell pepper slices (optional)

PREHEAT oven to 350°F. Spray 3-quart oval casserole with nonstick cooking spray.

CUT zucchini lengthwise in half. Cut crosswise into ¼-inch-thick slices. Combine spaghetti sauce, broth, zucchini, mushrooms and rice in prepared dish.

BAKE, covered, 30 minutes. Remove from oven and stir. Cover and bake 15 to 20 minutes or until rice is tender. Remove from oven; sprinkle evenly with cheese. Bake, uncovered, 5 minutes or until cheese is melted. Garnish with yellow pepper, if desired. *Makes 6 servings*

Baked Tomato Risotto

Creamy Vegetables & Pasta

1 can (10¾ ounces)
    condensed cream of
    chicken soup
1 cup milk
¼ cup grated Parmesan
    cheese
1 package (16 ounces)
    frozen seasoned pasta
    and vegetable
    combination
1⅓ cups FRENCH'S® French
    Fried Onions, divided

Microwave Directions:
Combine soup, milk and cheese
in 2-quart microwavable shallow
casserole. Stir in vegetable
combination and ⅔ *cup* French
Fried Onions. Microwave on
HIGH 12 minutes* or until
vegetables and pasta are crisp-
tender, stirring halfway through
cooking time. Sprinkle with
remaining ⅔ *cup* onions.
Microwave 1 minute or until
onions are golden.

Makes 6 servings

*Or, bake in preheated 350°F oven
30 to 35 minutes.

Tip: Add canned tuna or salmon
for a great meatless dish. Serve
with a salad on the side.

Lentil-Rice Casserole

2⅔ cups chicken or
    vegetable broth
¾ cup lentils, uncooked
¾ cup chopped onion
½ cup brown rice,
    uncooked
½ cup (2 ounces) shredded
    Swiss cheese
½ cup dry white wine
½ teaspoon dried basil
    leaves
½ teaspoon dried oregano
    leaves
½ teaspoon dried thyme
    leaves
⅛ teaspoon pepper
2 cloves garlic, mashed *or*
    ¼ teaspoon garlic
    powder
¾ cup SONOMA Dried
    Tomato Halves,
    snipped into strips
8 thin slices Swiss cheese

Combine all ingredients except
dried tomatoes and cheese
slices. Pour into ungreased 1½-
to 2-quart casserole. Bake,
uncovered, at 350°F for 1½ to 2
hours or until rice and lentils are
tender. Stir twice during baking.
Stir in tomato strips; top
casserole with sliced cheese
and bake 2 to 3 minutes more.

Makes 4 servings

Spinach Pie

1 tablespoon FILIPPO
    BERIO® Olive Oil
1 pound fresh spinach,
    washed, drained and
    stems removed
1 medium potato, cooked
    and mashed
2 eggs, beaten
¼ cup cottage cheese
2 tablespoons grated
    Romano cheese
Salt

Preheat oven to 350°F. Grease
8-inch round cake pan with olive
oil. Tear spinach into bite-size
pieces. In large bowl, combine
spinach, potato, eggs, cottage
cheese and Romano cheese.
Spoon mixture into prepared
pan. Bake 15 to 20 minutes or
until set. Season to taste with
salt.   *Makes 6 servings*

Golden Corn Pudding

2 tablespoons butter or margarine
3 tablespoons all-purpose flour
1 can (14¾ ounces) DEL MONTE® Cream Style Golden Sweet Corn
¼ cup yellow cornmeal
2 eggs, separated
1 package (3 ounces) cream cheese, softened
1 can (8¾ ounces) DEL MONTE® Whole Kernel Corn, drained

1. Preheat oven to 350°F.

2. Melt butter in medium saucepan. Add flour and stir until smooth. Blend in cream style corn and cornmeal. Bring to a boil over medium heat, stirring constantly.

3. Place egg yolks in small bowl; stir in ½ cup hot corn mixture. Pour mixture back into saucepan. Add cream cheese and whole kernel corn.

4. Place egg whites in clean narrow bowl and beat until stiff peaks form. With rubber spatula, gently fold egg whites into corn mixture.

5. Pour mixture into 1½-quart straight-sided baking dish. Bake 30 to 35 minutes or until lightly browned.

Makes 4 to 6 servings

Cheesy Rice Casserole

2 cups hot cooked rice
1⅓ cups FRENCH'S® French Fried Onions, divided
1 cup sour cream
1 jar (16 ounces) medium salsa
1 cup (4 ounces) shredded Cheddar or taco blend cheese

Microwave Directions:
Combine rice and ⅔ cup French Fried Onions in large bowl. Spoon half of rice mixture into microwavable 2-quart shallow casserole. Spread sour cream over rice mixture.

Layer half of salsa and half of cheese over sour cream. Sprinkle with remaining rice mixture, salsa and cheese. Cover loosely with plastic wrap. Microwave on HIGH 8 minutes or until heated through. Sprinkle with remaining ⅔ *cup* onions. Microwave 1 minute or until onions are golden.

Makes 6 servings

Sweet Potato Gratin

3 tablespoons olive oil,
    divided
2 cloves garlic, finely
    chopped
1½ pounds sweet potatoes
    (yam variety), peeled
    and sliced ¼ inch thick
⅔ cup chicken broth
    Salt
    White pepper
½ cup BLUE DIAMOND®
    Blanched Whole
    Almonds, chopped
½ cup fresh white bread
    crumbs
½ cup (2 ounces) shredded
    Swiss cheese
2 tablespoons chopped
    fresh parsley

Grease 8-inch square baking
pan with 1 tablespoon oil.
Sprinkle pan with garlic. Layer
sweet potato slices in pan. Pour
in broth. Season with salt and
pepper to taste. Cover and bake
at 375°F 30 minutes.
Meanwhile, combine almonds,
bread crumbs, cheese, parsley,
¼ teaspoon salt and ⅛
teaspoon pepper. Toss with
remaining 2 tablespoons oil.
Sprinkle over hot potatoes and
bake, uncovered, 20 minutes
longer or until top is golden.
Makes 4 to 6 servings

Tomato Scalloped Potatoes

1 can (14½ ounces)
    DEL MONTE® Diced
    Tomatoes, undrained
1 pound red potatoes,
    thinly sliced
1 medium onion, chopped
½ cup whipping cream
1 cup (4 ounces) shredded
    Swiss cheese
3 tablespoons grated
    Parmesan cheese

1. Preheat oven to 350°F.

2. Drain tomatoes, reserving
liquid; pour liquid into measuring
cup. Add water to measure
1 cup.

3. Combine reserved liquid,
potatoes and onion in large
skillet; cover. Cook 10 minutes
or until tender.

4. Place potato mixture in 1-
quart baking dish; top with
tomatoes and cream. Sprinkle
with cheeses.

5. Bake 20 minutes or until hot
and bubbly. Sprinkle with
chopped parsley, if desired.
Makes 6 servings

Prep Time: 8 minutes
Cook Time: 30 minutes

Green Bean Casserole

Ranch-Style White Sauce (recipe follows)
1 cup chopped onion
2 cloves garlic, minced
1½ cups sliced fresh mushrooms
1¼ pounds fresh green beans, cooked until crisp-tender
1 cup fresh bread crumbs
2 tablespoons minced fresh parsley

1. Preheat oven to 350°F. Prepare Ranch-Style White Sauce. Set aside. Spray medium skillet with nonstick cooking spray; heat over medium-high heat. Add onion and garlic; cook 2 to 3 minutes or until tender. Remove half of onion mixture. Set aside.

2. Add mushrooms to skillet and cook about 5 minutes or until tender. Combine mushroom mixture, beans and sauce in 1½-quart casserole.

3. Spray medium skillet with nonstick cooking spray; heat over medium heat. Add bread crumbs to skillet; spray top of crumbs lightly with nonstick cooking spray. Cook 3 to 4 minutes or until crumbs are golden. Stir in reserved onion mixture and parsley. Sprinkle bread crumb mixture over casserole. Bake, uncovered, 20 to 30 minutes or until heated through.   *Makes 6 servings*

Ranch-Style White Sauce

1½ tablespoons margarine
3 tablespoons all-purpose flour
1½ cups skim milk
3 to 4 teaspoons ranch salad dressing mix
¼ to ½ teaspoon white pepper

Melt margarine in small saucepan over low heat. Stir in flour; cook 1 to 2 minutes, stirring constantly. Using wire whisk, stir in milk; bring to a boil. Cook, whisking constantly, 1 to 2 minutes or until thickened. Stir in dressing mix and pepper.
          Makes 1½ cups

Green Bean Casserole

Creamed Spinach Casserole

2 packages (10 ounces
   each) frozen chopped
   spinach, thawed, well
   drained
2 packages (8 ounces
   each) PHILADELPHIA
   BRAND® Cream
   Cheese, softened
¼ cup milk
1 teaspoon lemon and
   pepper seasoning salt
⅓ cup crushed seasoned
   croutons

MIX spinach, cream cheese,
milk and seasoning salt until
well blended.

SPOON mixture into 1-quart
casserole. Sprinkle with crushed
croutons.

BAKE at 350°F for 25 to 30
minutes or until thoroughly
heated.

Makes 6 to 8 servings

Vegetable Cobbler

WESSON® No-Stick
Cooking Spray
1 medium butternut
    squash, peeled and cut
    into 1½-inch pieces
3 medium red potatoes,
    unpeeled and cut into
    1½-inch pieces
3 medium parsnips, peeled
    and cut into 1-inch
    pieces
1 medium red onion, cut
    into 6 wedges
¼ cup WESSON® Vegetable
    Oil
2 tablespoons chopped
    fresh dill weed, divided
1 teaspoon salt
¾ cup homemade chicken
    stock or canned
    chicken broth
1¼ cups milk, divided
1 (15-ounce) can pears, cut
    into 1-inch pieces,
    juice reserved
1 tablespoon cornstarch
4 cups broccoli florets
1 teaspoon grated fresh
    lemon peel
1¾ cups all-purpose baking
    mix
¾ cup shredded Cheddar
    cheese
½ cup cornmeal
¾ teaspoon coarsely
    ground pepper

Cobbler: Preheat oven to
400°F. Spray 13×9×2-inch
baking dish with Wesson®
Cooking Spray. In prepared
baking dish, toss *all* vegetables
except broccoli with Wesson®
Oil, 1 tablespoon dill and salt to
coat. Bake, covered, 40 to 45
minutes. Meanwhile, in
saucepan, combine stock, ½
cup milk, reserved pear juice
and cornstarch; blend well.
Bring to a boil. Add broccoli and
lemon peel and cook until
slightly thick; set aside.

Topping: In small bowl,
combine baking mix, cheese,
cornmeal, remaining 1
tablespoon dill, pepper and
remaining ¾ cup milk; mix with
fork until well blended.

Stir vegetables in baking dish.
Add pears; gently mix. Pour
broccoli sauce evenly over
vegetables. Drop 12 heaping
spoonfuls of topping evenly over
vegetables. Bake, uncovered,
for 15 minutes or until topping is
golden.   *Makes 8 servings*

Vegetable Cobbler

Hot Three-Bean Casserole

2 tablespoons olive oil
1 cup coarsely chopped onion
1 cup chopped celery
2 cloves garlic, minced
1 can (15 ounces) chick-peas, drained and rinsed
1 can (15 ounces) kidney beans, drained and rinsed
1 cup coarsely chopped tomato
1 can (8 ounces) tomato sauce
1 cup water
1 to 2 jalapeño peppers,* minced
1 tablespoon chili powder
2 teaspoons sugar
1½ teaspoons ground cumin
1 teaspoon salt
1 teaspoon dried oregano
¼ teaspoon ground black pepper
2½ cups (10 ounces) frozen cut green beans

*Jalapeño peppers can sting and irritate the skin; wear rubber gloves when handling peppers and do not touch eyes. Wash hands after handling jalapeño peppers.

1. Heat olive oil in large skillet over medium heat until hot. Add onion, celery and garlic. Cook and stir 5 minutes or until onion is translucent.

2. Add remaining ingredients except green beans. Bring to a boil; reduce heat to low. Simmer, uncovered, 20 minutes. Add green beans. Simmer, uncovered, 10 minutes or until green beans are just tender. Garnish with fresh oregano.
Makes 12 servings

Indonesian Honey-Baked Beans

2 cans (15 ounces each) white beans, drained
2 apples, pared and diced
⅔ cup honey
1 small onion, diced
½ cup golden raisins
⅓ cup sweet pickle relish
1 tablespoon prepared mustard
1 teaspoon curry powder or to taste
Salt to taste

Combine all ingredients in 2½-quart casserole. Add enough water just to cover. Bake at 300°F about 1½ hours, adding more water if needed.
Makes 8 servings

Favorite recipe from **National Honey Board**

Hot Three-Bean Casserole

Savory Scalloped Potatoes

1½ pounds all-purpose
potatoes, peeled and
thinly sliced
1 envelope LIPTON®
Recipe Secrets®
Savory Herb with
Garlic Soup Mix
1 cup (8 ounces) whipping
or heavy cream*
½ cup water

*Substitution: Use 1 can (12
ounces) evaporated milk and
eliminate water.

• Preheat oven to 350°F. In
lightly greased 2-quart shallow
baking dish, arrange potatoes.

• In medium bowl, combine
remaining ingredients; pour over
potatoes.

• Bake, uncovered, 45 minutes
or until potatoes are tender.
Garnish, if desired, with
chopped fresh parsley.

Makes 6 servings

Acknowledgments

The publisher would like to thank the companies and organizations listed below for the use of their recipes and photographs in this publication.

A.1.® Steak Sauce

Birds Eye®

Blue Diamond Growers®

Bob Evans®

Butterball® Turkey Company

Del Monte Corporation

EGG BEATERS® Healthy Real Egg Substitute

Filippo Berio Olive Oil

Florida Department of Agriculture and Consumer Services, Bureau of Seafood and Aquaculture

Guiltless Gourmet®

Healthy Choice®

Hebrew National®

Hormel Foods Corporation

Hunt-Wesson, Inc.

Kraft Foods, Inc.

Land O' Lakes, Inc.

Lawry's® Foods, Inc.

Lipton®

National Honey Board

Nestlé USA, Inc.

North Dakota Barley Council

Perdue Farms Incorporated

Reckitt & Colman Inc.

Sargento® Foods Inc.

Sonoma® Dried Tomatoes

StarKist® Seafood Company

Index

METRIC CONVERSION CHART

VOLUME MEASUREMENTS (dry)

1/8 teaspoon = 0.5 mL
1/4 teaspoon = 1 mL
1/2 teaspoon = 2 mL
3/4 teaspoon = 4 mL
1 teaspoon = 5 mL
1 tablespoon = 15 mL
2 tablespoons = 30 mL
1/4 cup = 60 mL
1/3 cup = 75 mL
1/2 cup = 125 mL
2/3 cup = 150 mL
3/4 cup = 175 mL
1 cup = 250 mL
2 cups = 1 pint = 500 mL
3 cups = 750 mL
4 cups = 1 quart = 1 L

VOLUME MEASUREMENTS (fluid)

1 fluid ounce (2 tablespoons) = 30 mL
4 fluid ounces (1/2 cup) = 125 mL
8 fluid ounces (1 cup) = 250 mL
12 fluid ounces (1 1/2 cups) = 375 mL
16 fluid ounces (2 cups) = 500 mL

WEIGHTS (mass)

1/2 ounce = 15 g
1 ounce = 30 g
3 ounces = 90 g
4 ounces = 120 g
8 ounces = 225 g
10 ounces = 285 g
12 ounces = 360 g
16 ounces = 1 pound = 450 g

DIMENSIONS

1/16 inch = 2 mm
1/8 inch = 3 mm
1/4 inch = 6 mm
1/2 inch = 1.5 cm
3/4 inch = 2 cm
1 inch = 2.5 cm

OVEN TEMPERATURES

250°F = 120°C
275°F = 140°C
300°F = 150°C
325°F = 160°C
350°F = 180°C
375°F = 190°C
400°F = 200°C
425°F = 220°C
450°F = 230°C

BAKING PAN SIZES

Utensil	Size in Inches/Quarts	Metric Volume	Size in Centimeters
Baking or Cake Pan (square or rectangular)	8×8×2	2 L	20×20×5
	9×9×2	2.5 L	23×23×5
	12×8×2	3 L	30×20×5
	13×9×2	3.5 L	33×23×5
Loaf Pan	8×4×3	1.5 L	20×10×7
	9×5×3	2 L	23×13×7
Round Layer Cake Pan	8×1½	1.2 L	20×4
	9×1½	1.5 L	23×4
Pie Plate	8×1¼	750 mL	20×3
	9×1¼	1 L	23×3
Baking Dish or Casserole	1 quart	1 L	—
	1½ quart	1.5 L	—
	2 quart	2 L	—